Coaching
and
Mentoring

Coaching
and
Mentoring

Practical Methods to Improve Learning

Eric Parsloe
and
Monika Wray

KOGAN
PAGE

London • Sterling (USA)

Scottish readers should be aware that, in order to simplify the text, the author has referred only to NVQs. In nearly every respect, these are the same as their Scottish equivalent, SVQs.

First published in 2000

Kogan Page Limited
120 Pentonville Road
London N1 9JN
UK

Stylus Publishing Inc.
22883 Quicksilver Drive
Sterling
VA 20166
USA

British Library Cataloguing in Publication Data

A CIP record for this book is available from the British Library.

ISBN 0 7494 3118 0

Typeset by Jo Brereton, Primary Focus, Haslington, Cheshire
Printed and bound in Great Britain by Clays Ltd, St Ives plc

Contents

Acknowledgements

All authors owe huge debts of gratitude to their partners, families and friends. We are no exception to this rule. We have tried to be specific in the text in identifying the other authors whose work or actual experiences have proved particularly informative. But perhaps our main sources of inspiration have been our fellow coach–mentors, clients, candidates and learners with whom we have worked over the past three years. They have willingly shared their learning experiences with us as well as giving us valuable feedback. As they are simply too numerous to mention individually, we hope that they will accept this general acknowledgement of their contributions.

Introduction

We met our deadline for completing this book on the 31 December 1999.

That dramatic date alone is an occasion to look back and to reflect, and then to look forward and speculate. The theme of reflection, conclusions and planing for the future is the essence of our book. It is, of course, also the widely accepted model of the way we learn as adults.

In our first chapter, 'From Marginal to Mainstream', we record how coaching and mentoring have developed as significant and increasingly widely used methods of helping and supporting people to learn more effectively. This development has occurred largely in the last decade of the last century. We believe that we are in the middle of a revolution of thinking about learning. By the end of the next decade, we suggest that coaching and mentoring will simply have become the normal way 'we do things around here'.

It is a very sobering reflection to realize how many learning experiences we authors have had in the last decade alone. Where have they all come from? The truth is, of course, that many of these experiences lie buried in our unconscious memories. Where it has been possible to identify the precise book, article, conversation or event we have acknowledged them with gratitude. But we are aware that much of our learning has come from the many hundreds of hours we have spent in one-to-one sessions as consultants, advisors, coaches and mentors. We have learnt too, often most powerfully, from the mistakes we have made. We were fortunate that our own coaches and mentors helped us to see these as learning opportunities rather than events that we should try to ignore or hide from in fear of blame.

The process of writing a book forces you to reflect on all these experiences and to declare the conclusions you have drawn. This we have attempted to do in a way that shares our understanding of what has worked well for us in practice.

Because we both like to base our actions on sound research and theory, we have also attempted to show these connections, too.

In Chapter 2, 'Helping People to Learn How to Learn', we show how recent research has led to new theoretical explanations of how we can learn more effectively. We argue that traditional methods need to be adjusted or, in some cases, abandoned in favour of coaching and mentoring as the 'preferred options'. This applies in particular to developing personal skills and learning to manage our own learning.

In Chapters 3 and 4, we deal in turn with the theory and practice of coaching and mentoring. As Chapter 4 – 'Mentoring: Where Theory and Practice Collide' – suggests, we recognize how important it is to relate theoretical models to specific situations so as to gain real, practical benefits.

Chapter 5 is titled, 'Community Mentors: The Catalysts for a New Profession'. This reflects our view that the recent developments in the community area provide the strongest endorsements of the power and effectiveness of coaching and mentoring as methods to help learning. It heralds too, the birth of a new profession of 'coach–mentors'.

We are acutely aware also, despite our years of learning experience, that other people's experiences and lessons may lead them to different conclusions. The excitement of living in an age of ever-increasing communication efficiency is that sharing different experiences has become so much easier. We know that, even as we complete our manuscript, new information and new experiences will become available that we wish had been available earlier, as they will almost certainly alter our thinking.

In earlier books we dealt with the age-old issues of giving feedback, observant listening and asking the right questions. When we came to write this book we thought there would be little new to add. We were wrong. In Chapters 6, 7 and 8, we have tried to capture new insights and relate new experiences drawn from recent coaching and mentoring sessions. Other writers' contributions have been valuable, too. Nancy Kliens's concept of the 'incisive question', is possibly the most powerful, partly from its simplicity.

We try to make the case for simplicity in Chapter 9, 'Managing the Relationship'. Coaching and mentoring are not new activities. They have been employed for centuries on an informal basis. What is new is the extent to which their power has been harnessed to meet the challenge of our ever-increasing need to learn new things in new ways. This has led to attempts to formalize the relationships. Research suggests that over-emphasizing the need to achieve perfect matching can be misguided. We suggest that there are 'Seven Golden Rules of simplicity' that should be followed to give the best chance of achieving the aim of helping people to apply practical methods to improve their learning.

Because learning is a continual process, we have included in Chapter 10 a suggested list of additional reading as well as the reference sources that we have used in our own research and learning.

Finally, we repeat the last three sentences of Chapter 9:

> Equally, it is worth emphasizing that our definition of the overall purpose of coaching and mentoring includes 'helping people to become the person they want to be'. This opens the possibilities of rewards from outside the immediate environment of the organizational setting. And, without becoming too idealistic, opens the possibilities also of meeting moral and spiritual fulfilment.

We hope you will share our enthusiasm for these possibilities, as well as the advantages of applying new learning methods to the day-to-day practicalities of life in the new century.

Eric Parsloe and Monika Wray
Oxford and London
31 December 1999

Chapter 1

From Marginal to Mainstream

At the start of the 1990s, you could hardly find a single book on either coaching or mentoring in the library of Templeton College – at that time Oxford University's only Management College. At the millennium, Templeton's librarian would now need a small transit van to carry all the books, journal articles, news stories and Internet references.

In the world of work and the broader social community, a rich variety of examples of successful applications of coaching and mentoring abound. It has truly been a transition from highly marginal activities to a mainstream focus of interest for professional teachers, corporate and community policy makers and those interested in people development. We are probably in the middle of an 'intellectual revolution' on these activities and it is not surprising that there is still confusion of definitions and language. By the end of the next decade coaching and mentoring will, we predict, have become so clearly defined and integrated into work and community life that it will be described routinely as simply 'the way we do things round here'.

In this chapter we attempt to sketch the 'big picture' review of the trends, developments and influences of this explosion of activity. We will start with the different influences on coaching.

The Academic 'Influencers'

Our own interest in the potential for both coaching and mentoring came from the management writers (who are largely from the US) of the 1980s. It was impossible to read the new thinking on issues like 'process re-engineering', 'total quality management', 'customer service excellence', 'employee empowerment' and 'the learning organization' without recognizing that the days of the traditional management science of command and control were numbered. Either implicitly or sometimes explicitly, like one of Blanchard's situational management styles, the notion of coaching began to enter the language of people management and development literature.

The US writer with probably the greatest early impact on the emerging profession of management coaching in Britain was Tim Gallwey in his *Inner Game of Tennis* (1974). The simple proposition that all great tennis players needed a coach to maintain their high levels of performance was a metaphor and message that was easy to relate to the management of people's performance at work.

Gallwey's philosophy that 'Performance = Potential minus Interference' was accompanied by the message that a coach's job was primarily to release the self-knowledge and potential that everyone possesses. The key to this was to develop greater self-awareness and a sense of self-responsibility in the performer. Again, these are messages that were in tune with the emerging new thinking about management and organizational performance.

The Sport Coach 'Influencers'

Not surprisingly perhaps, it has been the famous sports coaches turned management coaching gurus who have been the most visible group in shaping the early thinking and approaches to applying coaching to the workplace. Among the leading exponents were John Whitmore, former champion racing driver, David Hemery, former Olympic medalist and David Whitaker, former Olympic hockey coach. Towards the end of the decade, the former tennis player Myles Downey teamed up with The Industrial Society to form a 'School of Coaching' for high-flying managers, thus helping to consolidate the connection between sports coaching and a notion of 'best practice management'.

The medium most commonly used by this group to convey their messages are highly stimulating and memorable training courses, where practical examples of sports coaching are used to relate to the world of work. The analogy between high achievers in sport and work has fostered the belief that it is possible to develop 'great coaches' who can produce 'extraordinary results'. The key requirements, it is suggested, are simply the skills of questioning and feedback plus use of the GROW model (we'll explore this model in more detail in Chapter 3). The quite widespread notion that senior people should be the main recipients of coaching training is not unrelated to the undoubted success of this group in influencing expectations, attitudes and approaches.

However, John Whitmore's book *Coaching for Performance* (1997) remains an inspiring call for a change of management philosophy. However, like many pioneers before him, he has faced a growing number of other 'influencers' who challenge the sport coach approach.

The basis of some of the challenges is that the skills required to be a successful sports person are far narrower than those required to manage, for instance, a busy call centre, an intensive care ward of a large hospital or a pharmaceutical processing plant. Thus the approaches and techniques, it is claimed, are not easily transferred from one environment to the other. Suggesting that they can be simply results in raising false hopes and expectations.

Another challenge relates to the difference in motivation between sport, which has a combination of personal competitiveness and pleasure, and the world of work where many, if not most, people's motivation is a mixture of reluctance, fear and resistance to change. Apart from the natural high achievers therefore, it is claimed, the sports coaching approach often produces little real change in behaviour and performance. Most people don't aspire to be Olympic champions at work.

Despite the challenges, it remains true that this approach to work-based coaching continues to produce results that satisfy a particular segment of the market.

The Psychotherapy 'Influencers'

The profession of workplace counsellors is well established. At one end of the spectrum are the highly practical career counsellors. At the other end are the psychiatrists and psychologists who bring with them an aura of highly academically qualified professionals who understand how people function under stress. It was natural that this latter group should see the emergence of workplace coaching and mentoring as 'something we already do', although many would define workplace counselling as 'helping people to solve personal crises or to handle over-stressful situations' rather than managing their normal learning and development.

The techniques and approaches that this group of 'influencers' uses tend to be straight 'exports' from their previous work in the medical or social services environments. These are characterized by a belief that sessions need to be wholly client-centred and can last as long as necessary to achieve client satisfaction – anything up to half–a–day per session being considered normal. Their programmes are therefore usually expensive, which means that they tend to be confined to large organizations and then only to very senior people.

The term 'executive coaching' has become associated with this type of activity, and these coaches often use 360-degree feedback techniques or other personality profiling instruments to help with in-depth analysis. A common criticism is that the calibre and range of workplace experience of the 'executive coach' is often rather too limited. Using the term 'executive coach' can certainly make both the psychotherapist coach and their paymasters feel rather good about themselves. The serious practitioners in this group are very concerned to develop clear contracts of engagement with their 'clients' and agree codes of ethical practice with other professionals.

This approach can work extremely well for coping with the increased pressures and complexities of modern business life. However, by definition, it is not widely available, although it often provides good copy for journalists and therefore helps to create a rather misleading impression of the image of the nature and extent of coaching best practice.

The New-Life-People 'Influencers'

The 1990s have seen an upsurge in what we term 'new-life-people' thinking. This is not a very precise descriptive term, but it is intended to relate to a variety of quasi-philosophical groups who are keen to explore new and deeper understanding of their own personalities and how groups and individuals might learn and develop.

This approach seems to have a particular appeal to those involved in management and inter-personal skills training. 'Gestalt' theory and practice is one stream. The well-established transactional analysis enthusiasts are another. However, the most pervasive stream has probably been the NLP 'movement' – Neuro Linguistic Programming to give it the rather ugly and pretentious full title.

NLP has its origins in US fringe psychology and its advocates believe it has a particular relevance and application to coaching. NLP places an emphasis on understanding the implications of the language used during coaching relationships. It also claims to help people to focus on understanding how they cope with, and communicate to, themselves and others, about changes in behaviour. This may sound either very sophisticated or rather over-complicated depending on your preferences. The NLP coach may well attempt to communicate at a deeper and more meaningful level and for some people this produces valuable insights into opportunities for self-development. It will not, we suspect, be a popular approach for those wary of highly 'touchy-feely' initiatives.

Unquestionably, there exists a large number of practising coaches who find NLP techniques helpful and productive. There are also an increasing number of publications, conferences and events publicizing NLP and coaching and it can therefore reasonably claim to be an important 'influencer' on coaching philosophy and practice.

There is another group of 'new lifers' who are themselves heavily influenced by a particular brand of US writing and coaching practice. Laura Berman Fortang, the author of *Take yourself to the Top* (1999), is one example of a charismatic US advocate of 'personal life coaching', who has gained a following of enthusiasts for seeking new and alternative avenues for people to express themselves. Another (British) writer who belongs in this group is Eileen

Mulligan whose book is titled *Life Coaching – Change your life in 7 days* (1999). This promise has a feeling of over-exaggeration to us and can make people very wary indeed when accompanied, as it sometimes is, by high pressure marketing and selling techniques from the 'new lifers'. In a rapidly expanding market, you must expect a wide range of approaches to emerge even if they prove to be only short lived or remain a minority preference.

The Professional Trainer and Consultant 'Influencers'

The professional trainers and consultants are the group who you would expect to have the most significant influence on the way that coaching is being applied to the workplace – but they are not a homogeneous group.

Many trainers and consultants are under heavy time pressures and often feel that their top priority is to constantly impress and stimulate their client audiences. This leaves them open to the criticism that they are 'intellectual thieves and copycats' who simply read the latest textbook minutes before they have to perform. There would appear to be some justification in these claims in relation to coaching. It is clear that some have felt the need to jump on the coaching bandwagon by quickly renaming some of their existing interpersonal skills programmes as coaching.

Others have been seduced by the undoubted appeal and stimulation of the sports coaches and other 'evangelists' approach, and have either imported the star performers into their programmes or attempted to produce their own versions. Without the charisma and credibility of the star performers, the potential value of the coaching message delivered in this way is often diluted by this approach.

There also appears to be a very strong reluctance to break away from delivering training as a tutor/consultant-led classroom activity. This has meant that, in some organizations, coaching is being tarnished with the 'just another flavour of the month' criticism from people who find it difficult to apply the classroom-based experience to the operational realities of their own workplace. This is not however the whole picture.

Serious trainers and consultants have experimented with different models and approaches to fit the widely different situations where coaching might be applied. The differences between coaching to develop specific skills, for instance, and coaching for general self-development have been recognized. The need to match coaching styles and techniques to the different phases in an individual's job or career cycle is another area of study and experiment. New techniques are emerging, along with different coaching models, to be used as a key part of an organization's overall mix of learning and development activities. Some now advocate that coaching is 'the glue that makes traditional training stick'. Others, including ourselves, advocate that coaching (and mentoring) can properly be viewed as a 'preferred option' for developing personal skills and self-managed learning.

This is particularly true in relation to the increasing tendency for learning to be delivered electronically, either to the desktop or the home. Some people see these developments as a serious attack on social and community behaviour and dread the creation of a society of 'loners'. This attitude is often accompanied by a fervent belief that coaching has always to be a one-to-one and face-to-face activity. However, others are finding that electronic coaching can work quite well in certain situations and for certain people. Research and experiment are establishing that electronic coaching means relying mainly on the telephone and e-mail with which people are increasingly familiar in the workplace. Similarly, the use of Internet discussion groups is slowly beginning to be seen as a useful additional way of communicating. People are quite capable of adapting to new environments and the same will, we believe, undoubtedly be true for electronic coaching, too.

Trainers and consultants are great networkers and joiners. Coaching and mentoring philosophies encourage these tendencies and several small networks and groups have been established. The existing professional bodies will probably react to these pressures by forming 'special interest groups or sections' or risk the establishment of a separate professional organization.

As with all new professions, there will be growing pressure to establish standards of performance and behaviour. So far, this type of initiative has largely been met with help from government or European Community Social funding. The focus initially has naturally been on government-sponsored qualifications like National Vocational Qualifications (NVQs). We believe this approach will almost certainly prove to be inappropriate for this type of activity. The mainstream academic institutions will probably play an increasing role in meeting future demands for credible and nationally recognized standards that combine elements of performance evidence and academic rigour.

As the debate on the establishment of national standards gathers pace, the pressure to reach agreement on the precise definitions and language of coaching and mentoring will also increase. This is a convenient point to switch attention from the 'influencers' on coaching to the 'influencers' on mentoring.

Mentoring – The Semantic Jungle

Our early research in 1990 led us to develop a number of descriptions of mentoring activity and a definition of the difference between coaching and mentoring. The debate has continued at almost every gathering of practitioners we have attended over the past decade. At times, people have grown impatient and dismissed the debate as mere quibbling in a semantic jungle. We think a more accurate observation would be that the vast increase in activity under these headings represents the maturing of a new profession and that the debate is a healthy search for clarity of understanding.

We have not yet reached a consensus of terminology and we accept that our current terms and definitions may change again. For the moment however, we will continue to use the term 'influencers'.

The Professional Qualification 'Influencers'

The 'professions' have actively employed mentoring for many years as part of their professional qualification programmes. Some professions, like the Chartered Engineers, use the term 'mentor' explicitly. Others, like the Chartered Accountants, identify the role, but use the term 'counsellor'. Over the past decade, there has been little need for these bodies to change their thinking about the value of mentoring. Some, like the comparatively small Institution of Fire Engineers, have made mentoring more explicit in their qualification programmes as well as in their approach to lifelong learning generally.

The importance of continuing professional development is an increasingly highly organized aspect of many, but not all, professional bodies and the emphasis on mentoring is usually acknowledged. Continuing professional development is no longer confined to the individual professional bodies alone. The importance of this activity is now promoted and co-ordinated by a new Institute for Continuing Professional Development formed in 1998. This new

Institute certainly recognizes and intends to actively promote mentoring over the next decade.

The Vocational and Community 'Influencers'

In our early research, it was the emergence of the role of the mentor in connection with the new National Vocational Qualifications (NVQs) that led us to identify this group as potentially significant 'influencers'. We were correct, in the sense that the NVQ mentoring role has become well established, although NVQs themselves seem to have fitted into only one niche (created their own niche?) in the vocational qualification spectrum.

The role of the mentor has become central in the wider debate about vocational and lifelong learning as the key to access to, and involvement in, the world of work. Mentoring is now actively promoted as part of the government's Fair Deal at Work scheme, aimed at helping unemployed youngsters in particular to gain real jobs. There are schemes too for other disadvantaged groups, like one-parent families, which also aim to help people to learn how to join mainstream working life.

Underperforming school children (and schools) are now being offered the services of at least 1,000 full-time paid professional 'learning mentors' by the Department for Education and Employment (DfEE). The Home Office is sponsoring mentoring schemes to help people with drug, alcohol or other potential causes of crime or re-offending. Mentoring to help to tackle the issues of race, gender and cultural diversity are now sponsored by public money and also increasingly by employers, who recognize that these are issues that can adversely affect their economic performance. The Department of Industry has recently announced a programme to attract 1,000 volunteer business-to-business mentors, where senior executives from large organizations are invited to share their experience with small entrepreneurs in start-up businesses. A similar scheme, run by the DfEE, aims to recruit 3,000 senior executive mentors each year to help headteachers in a 'Partners in Leadership' programme.

Vocational and community mentoring is poised to have an enormous impact on 'the way we do things'.

However, it also raises issues of definitions. Is the vocational and community mentor intended to behave simply as a valuable, impartial friend and sounding board or should they also possess expert knowledge that they are required to share? Certainly, the NVQ mentor is required to impart expert information, so too is the one-parent family mentor. When a mentor is an expert advisor, are they not acting more as a coach than a mentor? What are the implications for perceptions of power and authority when a mentor is a paid professional as opposed to a volunteer 'friend'? These questions encapsulate the semantic debate.

The answer most often given currently is to ignore the search for a uniform definition and accept that what matters is that the *individuals involved in the activity understand clearly what the role means in their particular situation.* Our current research, however, has led us to the conclusion that it is more helpful to treat the emerging 'community' mentor as a distinctly different type of mentor and to recognize that the 'professional and vocational qualification' mentors have more in common with each other. We shall therefore be discussing three broad types of mentor in this book: 'vocational', 'community' and 'corporate'.

The Corporate 'Influencers'

Originally we termed this group the 'mainstream' mentors, but this is no longer an accurate description, as we have already discussed. However, mentoring in corporate life is still of vital interest to many, and is where the debate on the distinctions between workplace coaching and mentoring has particular relevance.

One of the most prolific writers on issues of corporate mentoring has been David Clutterbuck. He makes an important distinction between the US and European understanding of the concept of mentoring. He writes in his book, *Learning Alliances* (1998):

> Where you draw the line around mentoring depends on whether you adopt the traditional American definition of *career oriented mentoring* (having a powerful sponsor) or the European definition of *developmental mentoring* (where the prime focus is on personal growth and learning).

This is an important distinction and helps to explain why some of the earlier mentoring programmes in the UK tended to be focused on graduate development programmes in large multi-national organizations. Mentoring in corporate life now, however, embraces a wide range of individuals and situations, as we will see in Chapter 4. Our own research and experience support David's view that most UK corporate mentoring focuses on learning and we understand why he terms them 'learning alliances'. However, we are not happy to accept his definition of mentoring as an over-arching concept that relegates coaching (and numerous other roles) to a sub-set of mentoring. As we outline in subsequent chapters, both coaching and mentoring are processes that enable or support learning to happen. The important practical differences between them relate to the focus of the learning (short-term = coaching, or longer-term = mentoring) and to the power and authority relationships involved (direct management accountability or not). For many people interested in becoming practically involved in day-to-day mentoring these distinctions can cause unnecessary confusion. The real strength of coaching and mentoring is that they are both fundamentally very simple processes, and we now often use the term 'coach-mentor' to acknowledge the differences but avoiding over-complication. So once again the most sensible advice is still to ensure that the people involved in the specific situation and relationship know exactly what is expected of each other, irrespective of theoretical distinctions.

Crystal Clarity or Foggy Images?

The purpose of this chapter is to paint the 'big picture' so that the key issues can be discussed in more detail in the following chapters. However, is the picture painted so far clear or foggy?

As we believe that we are in the midst of a 'revolution in thinking' we are not surprised if there is still a good deal of fog rather than clarity. Where there is common agreement, we suspect, is that:

- coaching and mentoring are increasingly important and multi-faceted activities;

- coaching and mentoring each have a key role to play in helping to meet the learning and development needs of an increasingly complex and technology-dominated world of work and community living;

- while simplicity in day-to-day application is important, it is vital that policy makers and professional practitioners are aware of the nuances of the emerging language of the coaching and mentoring profession;

● the effective coach and mentor needs to have a good grasp of the processes, style issues and techniques involved as well as the necessary skills and attitudes.

It seems clear too, that applications and experiences of coaching and mentoring are likely to be different in different international and cultural environments and that we can all benefit from learning from each other. In that spirit, we end this chapter with a summary of the 'definition debate' prepared by Dr Rey Carr, one of Canada's most active writers on the subject. His views are presented as answers to the 'most frequently asked questions' from his mainly US contacts about role comparisons between mentors, coaches and therapists and are as follows:

General Purpose and Goal

Mentor	Most often orientated towards an exchange of wisdom, support, learning, or guidance for the purpose of personal, spiritual, career or life growth; sometimes used to achieve strategic business goals; content can be wide ranging.
Coach	Typically result – performance, success or goal-directed – with emphasis on taking action and sustaining changes over time; often used to improve performance in a specific area; more practice than theory driven; relies strongly on interpersonal skills.
Therapist	Usually problem or crisis-centred with emphasis on diagnosis, analysis or healing; might include testing, prescribed drugs, a focus on early life experience, involvement of other family members; typically grounded in extensive theory or philosophy.

Term for 'Other' Person

Mentor	Protégé, mentoree, mentee, partner or peer learner, learning group member.
Coach	Employee, co-worker or client.
Therapist	Patient or client.

Basis and Duration of Contact

Mentor	Can occur naturally, formally or informally; can last a lifetime or be part of a formal programme with a mutually agreed upon contract detailing meetings and other arrangements.
Coach	Often on an as-needed basis as identified by the client; when provided within a business, employee may receive coaching as part of a normal work role.
Therapist	Can range from short-term to long-term; client is typically free to discontinue at any time. Mandatory referrals can occur as part of a court or employer requirement.

Form and Nature of Contact

Mentor	Historically one on one; increasing use of one to group, peer group, e-mail, telephone and video.
Coach	Typically one to one; often provided by telephone and e-mail; peer-to-peer coaching used in education systems.
Therapist	Typically one to one or one to group; recent experimentation with Internet for one-on-one.

Life Skills and Experience

Mentor	Typically more extensive than, but may be similar to or diverse from, partner background; life stories of mentor often shared and influential.
Coach	Often involved in or previously associated with the same career area as client or employee; life stories of coach are for inspiration or education.
Therapist	May influence client choice, but often unrelated to outcome; typically only professional experience revealed; life story sharing depends on approach.

Training Necessary for Role

Mentor	Ranges from no formal training to limited hours in workshop format.
Coach	Often self-taught, increasing number of in-person and telecourses available.
Therapist	Typically has graduate degree with academic and clinical coursework.

Certification or Licensing

Mentor	Not required, but certificates and other forms of recognition typically provided in formal programmes.
Coach	Not required, but professional associations and some training organizations provide certification systems.
Therapist	Often required by legislation; practitioners belong to professional groups with code of ethics, insurance and peer review.

Compensation or Fees

Mentor	Strictly voluntary; published guidelines warn against any financial connections.
Coach	Most often coaching is part or all of workplace role; private coaches often paid by client on retainer basis.
Therapist	Typically paid by client or insurance on an hourly basis.

Role Value and Consensus

Mentor	Research basis moderate; anecdotal reports and personal experience are highly supportive and most frequent; high agreement on programme principles.
Coach	Highly practitioner driven; research basis minimal; testimonial of clients most frequent way to determine value; high agreement on principles/practices.
Therapist	Most researched role; often contradictory or controversial results; often difficult to determine value; wide variety of approaches and theories.

Learning and Feedback

Mentor	Relies on development of relationship; learning exchange increases over time, but can be minimized by hierarchy; all parties usually benefit from feedback.
Coach	Typically client-orientated with primary focus on client learning; coaches often solicit feedback to improve practice.
Therapist	Low level of mutuality; focus is exclusively on client; low possibility of therapist requesting feedback.

Chapter 2

Helping People to Learn How to Learn

It is a sobering thought to realize that up until the mid-1980s it was quite possible to be very successful in managing a business or community organization without even mentioning the word 'learning'. Certainly, that was our own experience. But for a growing number of people in the public and private sectors, the concept of the 'Learning Organization' is now seen as an accurate blueprint of the way organizations will need to be structured and to behave in the 21st century. The blueprint may be visionary, but each organization – small, medium or large – will, it is argued, need to build its own version if it is to be successful. Coaching and mentoring, we believe, will need to be an essential part of this blueprint.

The broad argument for the Learning Organization is that:

- we are moving into an era of global, information technology-driven organizations;

- success will depend on the speed with which new information is applied to current operations, problems and opportunities;

- storage, transfer and retrieval of information is essentially technology-driven, but application of that information is people-driven;

- applying information effectively means that people – and organizations – will need to learn to do things differently as a result of the new information;

- since new information is becoming continuously available, learning will need to be continuous for all organizations;

- only organizations, and individuals, that actively manage their learning processes will be successful – or indeed will survive!

The writers Mayo and Lank, in their book, *The Power of Learning* (1994), offer this definition:

> A Learning Organization harnesses the full brain power, knowledge and experience available to it, in order to evolve continually for the benefit of all its stakeholders.

A different perspective is offered by Peter Senge, who wrote in *The Fifth Discipline* (1992):

> Most of us, at one time or another, have been part of a great 'team', or group of people who functioned together in an extraordinary way – who trusted each other, who complemented each other's strengths and weaknesses and compensated for each other's limitations, who had common goals that were larger than individual goals and who produced extraordinary results. I have met many people who have experienced this sort of profound teamwork – in sports or in the performing arts or in business. Many say they have spent much of their life looking for that experience again. What they experienced was a learning organization.

Senge, who is credited as being one of the main architects of the concept of the Learning Organization, is pointing out that the unit of the small team or small business may be the best way to recognize how the Learning Organization works in practice. Successful large organizations may, of course, comprise a large number of small teams working coherently together towards a shared vision and common goals.

Senge's focus on the team in the world of sport and the performing arts also helps to highlight the potential role of the coach and mentor. Successful sporting and performing arts teams have long been associated with the high profile given to their coaches and mentors. These roles will be increasingly important in organizations that decide to become Learning Organizations.

There are other powerful forces operating, however, which are changing both the way organizations are structured and the way that they will increasingly behave. In most organizations there is constant pressure to reduce costs and maximize profits or give greater value for money for the services they provide. This had led to a widespread short-term focus on immediate results and constant efforts to reduce the numbers of people employed in organizations.

Flatter management structures, process re-engineering and excellent customer service initiatives are resulting in greatly increased pressures on people. It has also meant an end to the idea that people will have a job for life or a single career that is actively managed and developed for them by the organization for which they work. People will, therefore, have to become more responsible for managing their own careers and for continuous learning of new knowledge and skills if they are to remain 'employable'.

There is clearly a potential conflict between the needs for organizations to actively structure and manage the learning potential of their people and the pressures to change the nature of employment contracts towards a short-term 'only as we need you' basis. New attitudes and new techniques will have to develop to reconcile these conflicts.

Mayo and Lank suggest that these new philosophies and practices will be reflected in the development of new attitudes by 'model' employees of the Learning Organization. They express their view in what seems to be a 'credo':

- As an individual I do not expect the organization primarily to manage my career or my learning.

- I acknowledge that it is in my interest to enhance my personal value and to look after both my internal and my external continuing employability.

- I need a lot of support from my manager, who can allocate funds to me, empower me to manage my time between learning experiences and work achievements, and can be a coach to me in passing on his or her own experiences or help me through certain job-related experiences.

- I need the support of the organization as well.

- I want to be recognized for my increased value through learning.

- Both my manager and I can benefit from expertise in the management of learning from a specialist; and I need to be able to tap into databases of learning opportunities relevant to the organization I work in to enable me to make good choices.

The speed at which these kinds of attitudes, expectations and practices may develop is clearly debatable. The extent of the changes required should not be underestimated. In Britain, the culture of learning is dominated by the traditional method of its delivery over many decades, indeed generations.

Until their early 20s, an individual's learning is often perceived as being provided mainly by the state, free of charge. This has been followed in the world of work where the employer was seen to have taken on the responsibility for training the individual for their career. Managers have been part of this training culture as much as they have been part of the traditional culture of 'command and control' and hierarchical styles and structures. These attitudes combine to produce a powerful cocktail of resistance to change.

Transformation and acceptance of the very different attitudes, practices and structures required of a Learning Organization therefore will not be easy. Only those organizations that actively want to do so will make progress. The easy option for many currently successful organizations will be to remain passive or simply pay lip service to change while profits are made today. However, success, even in the short term it is argued, will only come to those who systematically tackle the new challenges posed by advocates of the Learning Organization.

Graham Guest has written extensively on this subject and advocates the importance of understanding how mental models can help us to understand complex new ideas. Discussing Senge's ideas, he writes:

- *Mental models* are deeply ingrained assumptions by which we make sense of the world. In a learning organization these models will always be challenged to discover whether they are the best representations of exactly what is happening at any one time.

- *Personal mastery* is the discipline of continually clarifying and deepening personal vision; it represents the learning organization's spiritual foundation.

- *Team learning* starts with dialogue, which in turn involves learning how to recognize the patterns of interaction in teams.

- *Building shared vision* involves adopting shared pictures of the future that foster genuine commitment rather than merely compliance.

- *Systems thinking*, Senge's fifth discipline, sees beyond isolated events into deeper patterns and connections; whereas event thinking is linear, systems thinking is cyclical, relying on constant feedback.

To these five disciplines, Guest suggests adding three complementary processes of:

> *Coaching* and *mentoring* that are often treated as synonymous or seen to overlap although it is helpful to distinguish between them, and *effective benchmarking* that helps the transfer of learning from one organization to another.

A Learning Organization could therefore be represented as in Figure 2.1.

Figure 2.1 *A model of 'The Learning Organization'*

The New Agenda for the Learning Organization

The concept of the Learning Organization produces an agenda for all types of organizations that includes:

- an increased focus on learning and development as the critical means of ensuring organizational effectiveness and sustainable competitive advantage;

- encouraging as many people as possible, and certainly all managers, to become coaches to ensure learning occurs in the workplace and elsewhere;

- establishing mentoring programmes to help to support learning;

- identifying the key personal skills necessary for individuals to operate successfully in a Learning Organization.

It will come as no surprise, therefore, that we offer the following definition of the overall aim of coaching and mentoring within the Learning Organization as:

> The aim is to help and support people to manage their own learning in order that they may maximize their potential, develop their skills, improve their performance and enable them to become the person they want to be.

Choosing How Best to Learn

Only a few lucky people find learning easy. One of the main reasons is that most of us have been used to being taught in pretty much the same standard way. We know that, given the chance, we prefer to choose to work in ways that suits us best. So, to make learning 'easier', why not help people to choose to learn in ways that suit them best? To do this, the coach–mentor needs to appreciate at least the basics of how we now understand the way that people learn. They might well start by examining their own approaches and preferences.

There is a great deal of research available on how adults learn best. Some writers suggest that there are three key questions you need to be able to answer before beginning to understand what approach might suit you:

- How do you perceive information most easily: do you learn best by seeing, hearing, moving or touching?

- How do you organize and process the information you receive: are you predominantly left brain, right brain, analytical or global?

- What conditions are necessary to help you to take in and store the information you are learning – the emotional, social, physical and environmental factors?

Other writers emphasize the differences in people's 'learning intelligences' or their ability to:

- speak and write well;
- reason, calculate and handle logical thinking;
- paint, take great photographs or create sculpture;
- use their hands or body;
- compose songs, sing or play musical instruments;
- relate to others;
- access their inner feelings.

One writer, Jenny Maddern, has captured the importance of understanding how the brain works in her illustrated booklet, *Accelerate Learning* (1994), when she emphasizes, in Figure 2.2, that:

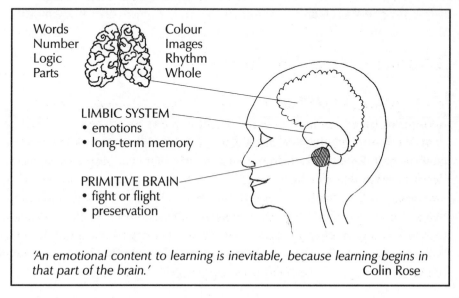

Words   Colour
Number   Images
Logic   Rhythm
Parts   Whole

LIMBIC SYSTEM
- emotions
- long-term memory

PRIMITIVE BRAIN
- fight or flight
- preservation

'An emotional content to learning is inevitable, because learning begins in that part of the brain.'   Colin Rose

Figure 2.2 *Learning needs to match the way the brain works*

Emotional Intelligence

As we have discovered more about the way the brain works, the more it has become clear that there is an important connection between learning and our emotions. This area of interest is frequently referred to as the theory of our 'emotional intelligence' which, it is claimed, is a far more accurate indicator of future success than the historical attachment to measuring IQ and classroom-based learning success. The theory has been credited to the US academics John D Mayer and Peter Salovey, although the science journalist Daniel Goleman is the best known writer on the subject. Mayer defines emotional intelligence as:

> The ability to perceive, to integrate, to understand and reflectively manage one's own and other people's feelings.

Understanding these 'intelligences', it is claimed, helps to explain why the traditional predominance of classroom-based education and training has so often failed so many people. Goleman's contribution has been to translate the wealth of academic research on the subject into language that the non-academic can understand. He has thus given credibility to the case for new and more sophisticated learning methodologies that practitioners have long understood, but have until recently failed to convince the policy makers to accept. Put simply, it is now possible to show scientifically why learning knowledge about facts, learning technical skills and learning personal skills each involve different parts of the brain and thus require different approaches and especially different time dimensions (*Emotional Intelligence*, 1996).

Learning Preferences

Clearly, there are a number of variables to consider when you begin to think about how you might learn more easily. Considering learning as *a process* offers some valuable practical insights.

Learning can be described as the process of acquiring new knowledge, understanding and skills. It is also believed to be a continuous cycle and the diagram below illustrates how people learn from experience. The process doesn't have a beginning, middle or end. Depending upon the learning situation, people can enter the cycle at any time. The most effective learning, however, will take place when you take the opportunity to complete all the stages in the cycle.

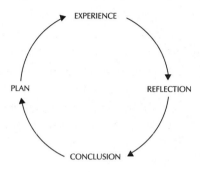

Figure 2.3 *The Learning Process*

EXPERIENCE	This is the actual learning experience. It may be: **Reactive** – something which happens to you, or **Proactive** – an experience which you deliberately seek out.
REFLECTION	A non-judgmental look back at what happened in the learning experience. This vital stage can be achieved quite quickly without seriously disrupting the work activity.
CONCLUSION	Drawing conclusions from the thoughts and notes made at the reflection stage to identify the lessons learnt.
PLAN	Planning and testing the lessons learnt from the conclusions, so that they can be related and applied to similar situations in the future.

Everyone will find some stages in this learning cycle easier than others. Your preference for a particular stage in the continuous learning cycle reflects your preferred *learning style*. Recognizing your own style, or combination of styles, will help you to select learning opportunities that suit your style best. Equally importantly, learning style analysis suggests what you may have to do to adjust your preferences to make the most of the learning opportunities that are actually available. Life does not always present us with options to do exactly what we choose.

Peter Honey and Alan Mumford are acknowledged UK experts and influential thinkers on the topic of learning styles. They have identified four learning styles, in their book, *Using Your Learning Styles* (1983) which link with the learning cycle, and they have characterized them in the following ways.

Activists (Experience)

● Activists are open-minded people, not sceptical. This tends to make them enthusiastic about everything new.

● Their philosophy is *'I'll try anything once'*; they tend to act first and consider the consequences later.

● They fill their days with activity; they tackle problems by brainstorming.

If you feel that you fit this description, then you are likely to learn best from activities where:

– it's appropriate to 'have a go';

– you get involved in short activities such as role-plays, and where you have the limelight;

– you are thrown in at the deep end;

– there is a lot of excitement and a range of changing tasks to tackle, usually involving people.

Reflectors (Reflection)

- Reflectors like to stand back and consider experiences, observing them from many different perspectives and listening to others before making their own comment.

- The thorough collection and analysis of data about experiences and events is what counts, so they tend to postpone reaching definitive conclusions for as long as possible.

- When they act, it is as part of a larger picture which includes the past as well as the present and others' observations as well as their own.

If you fit this description, then you are likely to learn best from situations where:

- you can stand back from events and listen and observe;

- you can carry out research or analysis;

- you can decide in your own time, and have the chance to think before acting;

- you have the opportunity to review what you have learnt.

Theorists (Conclusion)

- Theorists adapt and integrate observations into complex but logically sound theories, thinking through problems in a step-by-step way.

- They tend to be perfectionists who are uncomfortable unless things are tidy and fit into a rational scheme.

- They are keen on basic assumptions, principles, theories, models and systems thinking.

If you feel you are a theorist, you are likely to learn best when:

- you are intellectually stretched, ie through being allowed to question assumptions or logic;

- the situation has a structure and clear purpose;

- you can deal with logical, rational argument, which you have time to explore;

- you are offered interesting concepts, although they might not be immediately relevant.

Pragmatists (Plan)

- Pragmatists are keen on trying out theories, ideas and techniques to see if they work in practice.

- They positively search out new ideas and take the first opportunity to experiment.

- They like to get on with things and act quickly and confidently on ideas, being impatient with extensive discussion.

As a pragmatist, you are likely to learn best from situations where you can:

- use techniques with obvious practical benefits;

- implement what you have learnt immediately;

- try out and practise techniques;

- see an obvious link between the subject matter and a real problem or opportunity at work.

Many people have found these Honey and Mumford learning preference types both helpful and easy to apply (perhaps because they tend to simplify a much more complex set of explanations). We are not suggesting that people cannot learn from situations that do not suit their preferences, but experience has shown that people learn more effectively if they can choose learning opportunities that suit their preferred learning style(s).

Learning is most effective when you go through the whole learning cycle. This makes it important to develop each of these learning styles, so that you can successfully adapt your style of learning to take advantage of each stage in the cycle.

Your knowledge of these learning styles will help you to:

- recognize your preferred learning styles and those of your colleagues;

- design or seek out learning opportunities that will suit your preferred learning style;

- focus on developing your least preferred styles so that you can make the most of the learning cycle.

Many people have found that recognizing their own style is one of the most revealing and powerful pieces of information they can obtain. It often helps to explain many earlier problems with learning and gaining qualifications and, of course, it helps to highlight the differences between colleagues and friends, both in terms of learning and also in how they prefer to work.

Head and Heart

Taking responsibility for your own learning means learning at the level of both the head and the heart. Knowing what you think about an issue is only half of the story and, therefore, you have only learnt half of what there is to learn. Understanding how you feel about an issue is the second, and perhaps more difficult, half. Knowing what you think without understanding how you feel is like intellectually eating a meal: you don't really know what it tasted like and you're certainly not full.

Getting into the habit of treating yourself as a whole person will enhance your learning. Regularly asking yourself 'How do I feel about this issue?' and more important still, asking 'Why do I feel this way?' is a good discipline to get you started down the route of self-awareness and understanding, which is a basic building block for someone serious about learning. Remember, *learning has to have an emotional content because learning starts in that part of the brain*.

The Language of Learning

When you are trying to understand new ideas, apply new techniques or develop new attitudes at work, it can be very confusing indeed if key terms are defined in ways that can be interpreted differently by different people. This is certainly true with terms like 'learning', 'training', 'development', 'coaching' and 'mentoring'. While it is quite reasonable for organizations to choose their own definitions to suit their own situations, the reality is often that this clarity is not provided.

William Tute, writing in *People Management* (1995), the journal of the professional Institute of Personnel and Development, highlighted some of these issues:

> Training, education and development are close relations. Yet, in vital respects, training is the polar opposite of education and development. Consider first who owns the learning agenda, because that determines the effect the outcome has on the business's future.
>
> Take training: in its pure form, the learning agenda is someone else's. The direction is outside-in. Authority is top-down. Source material is an external view of best practice, whether set by national standards, a profession or trainer. The values are conformity and compliance.
>
> Compare this with education and development. The agenda is that of the learner. The direction is inside-out. Authority is bottom-up. Source material is the learner's untapped potential and the variety of values found in humankind. The values are challenge and change.
>
> Pilots learn to fly aircraft through the process of training. MBA students learn to manage the future through the process of education. The effect of training is convergence. The effect of education and development is divergence. Values, opinions, behaviour and culture are all affected. If we train MBA students and educate pilots, we are headed for a nosedive.

We have dealt with the language of 'learning', 'education' and 'training' in this section. We will be returning to the language of coaching and mentoring in Chapters 3, 4 and 5.

The Importance of 'Process'

The learning 'process' shows that people learn from experiences, whether they happen accidentally or are pro-actively sought, by attending a series of lectures, for example, or using an open learning module. As a result of these learning experiences, people reflect on them – consciously or unconsciously – and therefore draw conclusions that lead them to plan to act differently next time. This, in turn, leads to a new experience and thus the cycle begins again and indeed is likely to be a continuous process.

Development, on the other hand, is the 'process' of moving from one level of performance to a new and different level of performance. Development can be said to have occurred when a learner can demonstrate that he/she can perform consistently at the new level of performance. Development therefore implies the need for clear standards of performance and for methods of measurement or assessment against those standards.

The development process is also related to the state of mind or attitude of the performer. It is sometimes illustrated graphically, as in Figure 2.4:

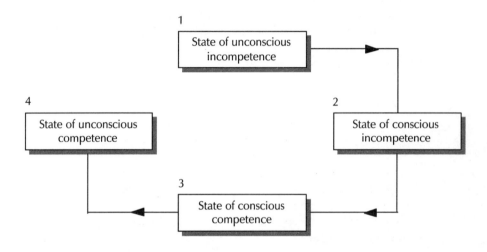

Figure 2.4 *The Development Process*

A popular example of this model is driving a car. At an early age, an individual may be completely unaware of the needs or techniques for driving a car, ie unconscious of the need for competence. As they enter their teens, people become aware of the need to pass a driving test with its clear standards of both knowledge and skill, ie they are conscious of their incompetence. After driving lessons and passing the test, people tend to drive in a very deliberate way, observing the rules and techniques they have been taught, ie conscious competence. After several years experience of driving, people tend to do it automatically to the standards required, ie unconscious competence.

Development can clearly be seen to be a progression from one stage to another. But what drives the development process is the learning of new knowledge, understanding, skills and behaviours. This can be illustrated graphically as in Figure 2.5:

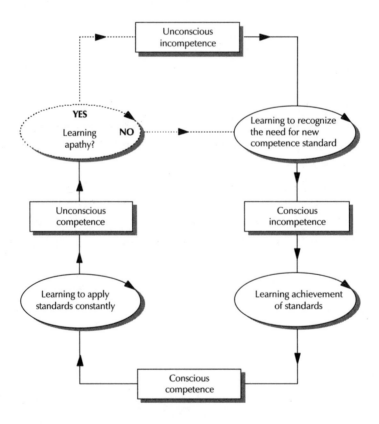

Figure 2.5 *The Learning and Development Processes*

Seen in this way, it is clear that different learning needs exist and different learning techniques are required at different stages of the development process to drive individual performance to higher levels.

It also illustrates the very real change that can occur when someone reaches a prescribed level of performance and operates with unconscious competence. Apathy and complacency can set in and this is often described as the 'comfort zone'. The task for the coach and mentor is to be able to recognize all the stages of the development process and the related learning needs and, in particular, the importance of avoiding the learning apathy or unconscious incompetence stage.

In a Learning Organization, people will have been convinced of the continual need to move from their current standards of performance to higher levels and that continuous learning is the key to continuous improvements in performance. It is a key role of the coach and mentor to help to maintain the focus on learning opportunities and benefits.

Learning Inefficiencies

Alan Mumford in his book *Effective Learning* (1995), highlights the main reasons he sees for learning inefficiencies. We believe that these can be organized as a continuum ranging from failures of perception to failures of implementation. Our interpretation is shown in Figure 2.6.

A successful coach or mentor therefore needs to understand the range of factors that influence a learner's perception of learning opportunities as well as the factors which influence the effective implementation of those opportunities. Motivational factors are also critical. We'll look at each of these in turn.

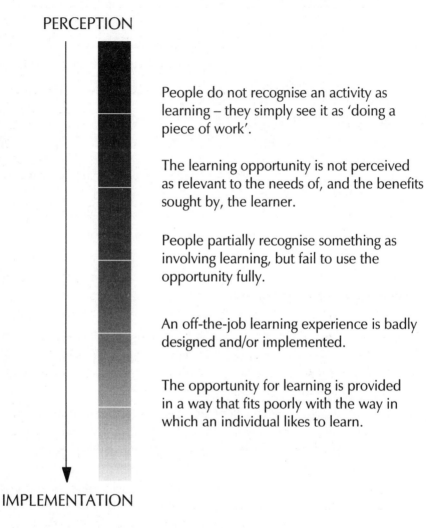

PERCEPTION

People do not recognise an activity as learning – they simply see it as 'doing a piece of work'.

The learning opportunity is not perceived as relevant to the needs of, and the benefits sought by, the learner.

People partially recognise something as involving learning, but fail to use the opportunity fully.

An off-the-job learning experience is badly designed and/or implemented.

The opportunity for learning is provided in a way that fits poorly with the way in which an individual likes to learn.

IMPLEMENTATION

Figure 2.6 *A Five Point Scale of Learning Inefficiencies*

Perception of Opportunities

The first step in developing an accurate perception of learning opportunities is to establish that a real need to learn exists.

Some people may be genuinely unaware that they need to learn anything new at all. Once a need has been recognized, it is likely that previous experiences of learning will significantly affect perceptions. People who equate learning only with the classroom or training course will have a limited vision of learning opportunities and will need to be made aware of many opportunities for learning that exist in the workplace. Past experiences of learning – particularly if they were negative – will also have a powerful influence.

It is probably true to say that most people are only vaguely aware of the learning process and are therefore quite likely to miss opportunities.

This is particularly true when it comes to recognizing the valuable opportunities to learn from mistakes. All too often, mistakes are associated with blame and denial and are quickly passed over and forgotten. The culture of the organization is important in this respect. If the prevailing organization culture is one of blame and fear, then perception of learning needs and opportunities is likely to be correspondingly low. Similarly, if the structure and nature of a job is restrictive, repetitive and boring, it is more difficult to stimulate enthusiasm for on-the-job learning. Creating a genuine and active learning culture around a learner's current job is a key task of the modern coach and mentor.

Implementation of Learning Opportunities

Assuming a reasonably high level of awareness and perception of learning opportunities, learning effectiveness can be significantly influenced by the possibility or reality of the way the opportunities are implemented. For instance:

- A learner may imagine that a range of opportunities exists for them but in reality these may not actually be easily available or affordable.

- The impact of the line manager and colleagues may also influence the implementation of opportunities. The line manager who pays only lip-service to the need for learning will often find reasons to deny access or adequate time.

- Operational pressures from colleagues and direct reports may also lessen a learner's willingness and ability to seize relevant opportunities.

- The quality of the coach, mentor, trainer or facilitator will have a powerful influence on the quality of the learning experience.

- Learners themselves may have blockages to learning of which they may be unaware. This is particularly true of what are called 'defensive barriers' when for reasons of status, prestige or pride, a learner unconsciously fails to take maximum advantage of a learning opportunity.

- Blockages to learning may come from the learning methods employed. The learning design or technology used may simply be inappropriate to the content.

- The learning institution itself may be inappropriate – a college environment might be unsuitable for a programme for high flying marketing executives, or an Outward Bound course inappropriate for learning basic financial management techniques.

- The method of assessing and evaluating performance, progress and results can also be critical. An obsession with passing a test to gain a qualification can be a block to developing a wider understanding of a subject or skill.

An awareness of these 'implementation factors' is crucial if the coach and mentor are to help to avoid learning inefficiencies.

The Learner's Motivation

An individual's desire to make the most of learning opportunities is often influenced by their perception of the rewards and punishment involved. 'The more you learn, the more you'll earn', for example has become a recognized phrase. A person's social and career successes to date, as well as their future aspirations and vision, are also important motivational influences. These perceptions will clearly be different for individual people at various stages of their careers.

Research evidence suggests, however, that learners are motivated most effectively by the interest, enjoyment, satisfaction and challenge of the learning process itself rather than simply by the rewards and punishments related to learning. The former factors are termed 'intrinsic' motivators, the latter 'extrinsic' motivators.

As we have already seen, individual learning style preferences and learning capabilities each have a bearing on a learner's motivation. Faced with opportunities that do not appeal or which seem too difficult, a learner's motivation is likely to be low.

Finally, an individual's self-confidence and general personality has to be taken into account. Building self-confidence, self-awareness and self-esteem are a critical part of the modern coach and mentor's role. The higher the levels of confidence, awareness and esteem, the higher the learner's motivation to seize learning opportunities and to take responsibility for improving their levels of performance will be.

The challenge for the modern coach and mentor is first to recognize the interrelated influences in the 'learning matrix' and then to identify techniques, tactics and skills to handle them. Figure 2.7 illustrates the range of influences that have to be managed by the successful coach or mentor.

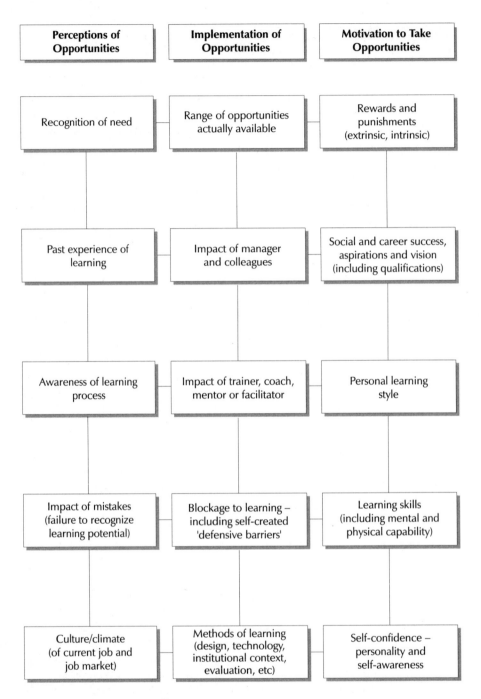

Perceptions of Opportunities	Implementation of Opportunities	Motivation to Take Opportunities
Recognition of need	Range of opportunities actually available	Rewards and punishments (extrinsic, intrinsic)
Past experience of learning	Impact of manager and colleagues	Social and career success, aspirations and vision (including qualifications)
Awareness of learning process	Impact of trainer, coach, mentor or facilitator	Personal learning style
Impact of mistakes (failure to recognize learning potential)	Blockage to learning – including self-created 'defensive barriers'	Learning skills (including mental and physical capability)
Culture/climate (of current job and job market)	Methods of learning (design, technology, institutional context, evaluation, etc)	Self-confidence – personality and self-awareness

Figure 2.7 *The Learning Efficiency Matrix*

Training Inefficiencies

Coaching and mentoring have now become the third most frequently used approaches in the UK corporate learning armoury, after on-the-job-training and the traditional training course. Viewing them as just another weapon in the learning mix may suit some organizations. For others, they may provide what some people describe as the 'essential glue that makes training courses stick'. What they are referring to is that coaching and mentoring programmes can provide an ongoing and one-to-one opportunity to reinforce and apply the learning that occurs in a typical classroom-based training course. As with Goleman's popularizing of emotional intelligence, so coaching and mentoring may now be the 'popular' answer to deficiencies that have long been known to exist with traditional training methodologies.

In the last century, research by Ebbinghaus the German psychologist produced results, validated since by scores of other research, that showed that '90 per cent of what was learnt in a class was forgotten within 30 days and 60 per cent was forgotten after 1 hour'. Roy Harrison, the Institute of Personnel and Development's Policy Advisor, reported recent US research which showed that *on average* only 10-20 per cent of learning through training transfers into people's work (Harrison, 1998). Other surveys have shown that more than half those attending training courses felt that 'they already knew most or quite a lot of the content', a third felt that 'the training made no difference at all to their performance' and only 2 per cent felt that 'the training had broken new ground'.

With our current level of understanding about how people learn, the main explanation for these types of deficiencies is most probably the application of the outdated traditional uniform approaches of delivering learning.

Daniel Goleman (1996) bases his criticisms of these traditional methods on what he sees as the widespread failure to appreciate the implications of emotional intelligence theories. He claims:

> People have not made a clear distinction in training methodologies between kinds of abilities, technical skills and the domain of personal abilities, that I call emotional intelligence. But the brain does... Emotional intelligence, unlike the cognitive and technical skills, entails a more primitive part of the brain – the limbic centres or the emotional brain. The emotional brain learns differently from the neo-cortex, where technical skills and cognitive abilities reside. The neo-cortex

learns fine in the classroom model, or from a book or from a CD ROM. In other words, it learns quickly, it can learn in a single trial, its mode is associational. It ties new knowledge to an existing network and that happens very quickly in the brain.

The emotional brain learns in a completely different mode, through repetition, through practice, through models. In other words, it learns through a model which is that of habit change. That being the case, people need a certain set of elements in a training approach if it is going to be effective.

It should come as no surprise therefore that we advocate that, for certain topics (like personal skills), coaching and mentoring are most sensibly seen as 'preferred options' in helping people to learn.

Helping people to learn how to learn is the main aim of the coach and mentor. It is clear that new approaches to learning are essential. It is also clear to us that the definition of learning merely as a process does not really suit its overall importance in our emerging society. We therefore offer the following definition:

Learning is both a process and a continuous state of mind, which transcends all traditional organizational boundaries and structures, and has become a central feature of the way we live.

Chapter 3

Coaching: Theory and Practice

We think it would be helpful to deal with the theory of coaching first and then discuss a number of examples of coaching in practice.

We have established that coaching is a dynamic and expanding workplace activity. For our purposes it is necessary to discuss the ideas and theories of an ideal coaching model and, at the same time, recognize that every coach is likely to behave in the way that seems appropriate to them in their particular situation. Describing an ideal model therefore is not to say 'This is the only way to coach', but rather 'This is a benchmark to compare your real-life practice to'.

It is probably true that each definition proposed by any of the recent writers on coaching can be said to accurately describe what happens in practice in many day-to-day situations in 2000. Organizations have been moving at different speeds towards more sophisticated and effective implementation of coaching. The most important point, however, is not that everyone has to agree on a single definition, but that everyone in a specific organization should know the definition that applies to their particular situation.

One of the most colourful definitions is proposed by our colleague Myles Downey in his book, *Effective Coaching* (1999):

> Coaching is an art in the sense that when practised with excellence, there is no attention on the technique but instead the coach is fully engaged with the coachee and the process of coaching becomes a dance between two people moving in harmony and partnership.

The definition we have become most comfortable with is somewhat less exotic:

> Coaching is a process that enables learning and development to occur and thus performance to improve. To be a successful coach requires a knowledge and understanding of the process as well as the variety of styles, skills and techniques *that are appropriate to the context in which the coaching takes place.*

We are aware that our preference for focusing first on the process of coaching is not shared by some coaching theorists, who prefer to emphasize the interpersonal skills aspects of the coaching relationship. Our experience suggests that it is more helpful first to understand exactly 'what' a coach is supposed to do before moving on to understand 'how' it should be done. Superb skills applied in a haphazard way are unlikely to be a recipe for success.

Coaching as a Process

Coaching, like all processes, requires each stage to be properly completed if the whole process is to work successfully. Missing out stages or concentrating on just one stage at the expense of the others can lead to confusion and poor results. The coaching process can be illustrated simply in the diagram on page 43.

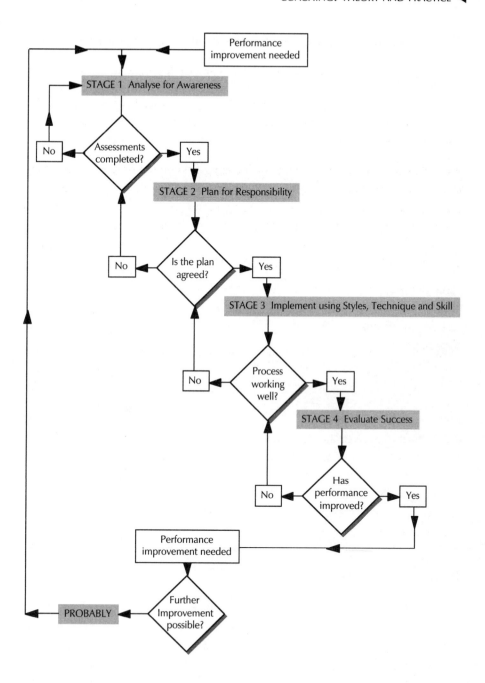

Figure 3.1 *Coaching Process Model*

Each stage is described in more detail in the following paragraphs.

Stage 1 Analysing for Awareness

Coaching can only start when the learner develops an awareness of the need to improve their performance or change the way they have been doing things. Without a genuine recognition of need, it is almost impossible to change behaviour. The coach has to help the learner develop this awareness because, in the same way that you can take a horse to water but you can't make it drink, you cannot coach someone until they actually want to be coached.

Learners develop awareness in a number of ways, but probably the best way is by analysing their current performance and comparing it to the level that they would like to move towards. Having clear standards, or performance competences, to aim for is clearly very helpful particularly when coaching to develop a specific skill. Using a self-assessment exercise as the basis for a subsequent discussion with the coach is a powerful technique for developing awareness.

At this stage it is also important to check the learning style preferences of both the learner and the coach. For the learner, this will provide insights into ways of learning that they will naturally prefer and therefore probably find easier and more enjoyable. For the coach, it is important to recognize any differences in preferences between themselves and the learner. This will help to guard against the natural tendency to suggest learning opportunities that work well for them but which may be inappropriate for the learner. It will also help to spot situations where any obstacles to learning may be caused by the learner's choice of methods rather than the inherent difficulty with the content of the learning.

Stage 2 Planning for Responsibility

It has long been argued that effective learning and development only really occur when the individual takes personal responsibility for the outcome. The planning stage of the coaching process is the opportunity for the learner to begin to exercise responsibility. There is a temptation to ignore this stage, particularly if the coach or learner has an activist learning style preference and is impatient to 'get on with it'. Busy managers are also inclined to ignore this stage and often prefer the informal 'let's do it on the run' approach.

The danger of missing out on this stage is that the coaching can become *ad hoc*, ie unstructured and failing to focus on the real issues. If self-managed learning is the preferred approach, then planning is absolutely vital.

Coaches cannot, and should not, attempt to impose learning programmes. Learners must be actively involved in the decision making. Some compromises between an ideal programme of learning and what can realistically be afforded will often be necessary. However, experience suggests that agreeing a Personal Development Plan (PDP) of some kind with their manager ensures that the necessary time and space in the working day will be made more readily available.

A successful PDP needs to answer these key questions:

- What is to be achieved?
- How will it be done?
- Where will it be done?
- When will it start and end?
- Who will be involved?
- Who needs to agree the plan?

In many organizations, individuals are already encouraged to have PDPs. In a minority of instances, the PDPs cover any topic that interests the learners because the organization judges that encouraging the development of the learning habit is more important than precisely what is learnt. Few organizations are likely to follow this enlightened approach, however, and most will probably insist that a PDP is clearly linked to business objectives as well as to individual aspirations.

To be most effective, a coaching PDP (unlike the traditional annual appraisal PDP that is often in practice only a long wish-list) should focus on only one or two specific development goals over relatively short time frames, perhaps only the next three months. It is important too, that any development goal in the PDP should be SMART: specific, measurable, achieveable, relevant and time-framed. This simple mnemonic is often only paid lip service in practice, but it can be a very powerful technique for ensuring real focus. The PDP should be reviewed at least on a monthly basis and thus become an integral part of the performance management process.

Stage 3 Implementing the Plan, Using Styles, Techniques and Skills

Coaches need to use implementation styles and techniques *that are appropriate to the situation in which the learner is operating*. The appropriate style and technique also need to be employed with the right balance of personal coaching skills. The most important of these skills are probably giving feedback, observant listening and effective questioning. We will be looking at several coaching techniques as well as these skills in more detail later.

Opportunities for coaching arise on many different occasions during the working day and it is important to seize them when they occur. This leads some people to argue that there is little need for formal planning, and that the best coaching is informal and relies almost entirely on questioning and immediate feedback.

Our experience suggests, however, that creating awareness and a sense of personal responsibility requires time for proper planning, if genuine development is to be achieved. The two approaches are in fact complementary, while formal awareness and planning are important, informal coaching should take place whenever the opportunity arises.

Our main concern about the informal approach to coaching is that it very often leads to *no coaching at all* once the initial enthusiasm wears off. The most common reason for coaching not happening is that people fail to find the time to do it. A more formalized approach that sets aside an hour a week or month in both parties' diaries is much more likely to ensure it happens. Formalized time tabling may sound boring, but in a hectic working environment it often produces results, especially when the manager has already signed off the PDP. Formality also often ensures regular opportunities to monitor and review progress on the PDP and to reinforce new learning.

Stage 4 Evaluating for Success

Many coaches confuse monitoring with evaluating. Monitoring is the essential activity of regularly checking that progress is being made in implementing the PDP. Evaluating is the activity of reviewing the PDP once it has been completed. It is a one-off activity involving the coach and the learner.

The key questions are:

- Were the development goals achieved?

- Did the different components of the PDP work in the sequences they were designed to?

- What changes, if any, were made to the PDP and why?

- Was the PDP cost-effective?

- Were there any unexpected benefits?

- What would you do differently next time?

- Is there a need for a new PDP to improve performance still further?

It is clear that if the answer to the final question is 'Yes' (which it probably will be as performance needs to improve continuously), then the whole coaching process needs to start again.

Coaching Styles

Style describes 'the manner in which the coaching is performed', although some writers (inappropriately in our opinion) use the term 'style' to describe different roles or types of coaching. However, we believe that there is a more helpful and all-embracing definition of style in the same way that there are understood to be various learning or working styles. However, these are not based on a psychological analysis of the coach. Coaching styles are based on a continuum that ranges from situations where the learner is completely inexperienced to situations where the learner is highly experienced and capable.

When coaching inexperienced learners, the appropriate coaching style may be termed the 'hands-on' style. Where learners are highly experienced, the style is termed the 'hands-off' style. In between the two extremes is a variety of styles that the coach needs to be able to adopt, *depending entirely on the level of experience and performance of the learner.* With someone who is completely new to a situation or needs to develop a specific new skill, it may be entirely appropriate for a coach to adopt a hands-on, almost instructor-like, style. When dealing with an experienced high performer, like an Olympic athlete or Chief Executive, it is more appropriate to adopt a hands-off style and rely mainly on questioning and feedback skills. Experience shows that the more rapidly a coach can move from a hands-on to a hands-off style, the faster improvement in performance will be achieved. The simple explanation for this is that as you move along the continuum towards hands-off, the more control and responsibility is transferred from the coach to the learner.

A Sporting Analogy

Carolyn Robertson is a former regional sales manager from the pharmaceutical industry and, latterly, a management consultant. She describes herself as 'an enthusiast about work, but passionate about eventing'. This is her report of her experience.

Carolyn not only enjoyed her chosen sport – one-day eventing – a great deal, but she soon realized that she had the potential to try and compete at the highest level. Recognizing the need for specialist coaching, she turned to an experienced horse-riding trainer for help. Steady progress was made over a five-year period and she was achieving modest success in competitions, but gradually her coaching yielded fewer and fewer improvements.

In an attempt to improve, a change of horse was recommended, but still no results. She became frustrated and lacking in self-confidence. Her relationship with her coach became strained and she began to give up her ambition of being successful at eventing. Finally, she decided to change her coach in a last attempt to rediscover her form.

The new coach introduced very different learning methods and, after only a few weeks, significant progress was being made. The new approach was very much a hands-off style of coaching. It began with a four-day assessment of horse and rider, both together and individually. An action plan divided into stages was agreed. Each stage was completed when the agreed level of competence was reached. Carolyn was asked to keep a diary of all activities, thoughts and self-analyses which she then brought to the session for discussion. The emphasis here was on self-reflection that, apart from being a valuable exercise in itself, also saved time. Carolyn says:

> I now realize that, when lack of progress becomes evident, time must be taken to analyse and explain the cause. Through discussion, a plan of action should be agreed.

These new and more formal coaching sessions were structured around a series of key questions:

- What are you trying to achieve and is that what you are achieving?

- But what about trying…?

- What are you going to do now to get where you want to be?

- Would you let me tell you what I feel about it?

Forcing Carolyn to focus on what her real objectives were in this style encouraged her to take responsibility for everything that happened.

However, like most real-life coaching situations, there were times when such a single coaching style was not always appropriate. For example, a much more hands-on role was adopted when tackling new or particularly difficult areas. When this was the case (perhaps in relation to a particular manoeuvre), explanations of what was needed and how it could be done were given by the coach. Carolyn would first try the movement on her own; the coach would then demonstrate what was happening and what should be happening. Carolyn would copy the coach and then repeat it on her own, and they would return to the problem area at the end of the session to check the earlier learning had been retained.

During all coaching sessions, though, continuous evaluation and assessment were taking place with time frames and short-term goals constantly being set and reset in the light of progress. It was vital that success and achievement were recognized. Carolyn was also inspired to spend time researching the theory of successful riding, which she saw as part of her own self-coaching development.

Apart from finding this type of coaching enjoyable and challenging, Carolyn found her confidence had increased. She had a deeper understanding of processes and the causes of mistakes. Most importantly, she became able to take corrective action of her own accord. This was in stark contrast to her previous experience of coaching when she felt she had not been taken seriously or given 100 per cent attention by her coach. On reflection, she feels this might have been because she was seen as a threat by him as she became better than he was. She now believes:

> The pupil must feel that the coach has confidence in his or her abilities. Coaches must take into account the pupil's experience but, at the same time, not make assumptions, especially if the pupil's circumstances change.

Her new coach, it seems, had found the right balance. As well as having the right technique, Carolyn also believes that the coach's attitude is vital to success:

> The pupil must feel able to ask the most basic of questions, which means no coach should put themselves out of reach physically or intellectually. Honesty, trust, empathy and respect are key words in any coaching partnership.

After five years, Carolyn clearly needed to be taking an important step forward in her coaching. While she recognized that almost any change at that time would have helped, the new methods that are more appropriate to her experience, ability and preferred learning style have helped her enormously.

It is clear, too, that Carolyn's coach, perhaps unconsciously, was following many aspects of our suggested ideal coaching model.

More Examples from Performers

Joan Sutherland, the Australian opera singer, actually married her coach! She met Richard Bonynge in 1951 when she entered the Royal College of Music. He was doing advanced study at the time. He spotted her great talent and began to coach her. At first this was in the form of friendly advice, but gradually it became more and more formal. One famous coaching technique he used to develop and extend her voice, was to sit at the piano in a position where she could not see the keys. By getting her to copy the notes he played, he took her beyond her imagined limit of high C! They married on 16 October 1954.

David Hemery, the former Olympic 400m hurdles champion, has spent many years researching, developing and practising coaching in sport and business. He has a fund of interesting stories. He compares his own gold medal track performance at the Mexico Olympics in 1968 with that of Lyn Davies in the long jump at the same Games. Both were superbly fit and had received extensive coaching.

Davies had won the gold medal at the previous Olympics in Tokyo. He knew his main competitors and their potential performance well. He was also intensely competitive and felt he could beat them. He was proud of his will to win the gold again. That was his focus. Almost as soon as the competition began, Bob Beamon, a little-known US athlete, produced a jump that not only beat the world record but exceeded everyone's expectations of what was possible. Davies knew he couldn't beat it. His confidence evaporated. He finished last, producing a below average performance. He had set himself no other goal other than to win.

Hemery and his coach on the other hand had planned his approach meticulously for months. The schedule included milestones for qualifying times, team selection, positioning in the heats and the semi-finals. Hemery wanted to win the gold. He calculated that to do so, he had to run faster than anyone had run before. That became his goal in the final. That is how he ran the race. He exceeded his performance goal, won the race – and also the gold medal which had been his ultimate goal.

The importance he and his coach placed on planning a schedule and clear goal-setting was confirmed. This is also vital in the work situation. Involving your boss in the process is important, too. Only if management agree with the time required and with the goals to be achieved will they allow the space for the coach and learner to work.

Examples from the Workplace

John Bailey is a Development Advisor with the accountants KPMG. He has identified the following best practice points:

- In situations where coaching is being undertaken for a particular role, it is important that there is an exchange of expectations.

- It is critical that the principle of coaching is to help people to help themselves and that it does not create a dependency on the coach.

- Coaches must have excellent listening and questioning skills and be able to respect confidences.

Cameron Burness, a production plant manager with ICI Pharmaceuticals, fully believes that coaching is an integral part of management. He is always on the look-out for coaching opportunities:

I don't actually need to be a technical expert in everything that my 100 or so staff might be doing. Being able to listen and ask the right questions, to understand a problem quickly and give positive feedback is what I see as my coaching responsibility. I find the experience–reflection–conclusion–action loop to be a sound method to follow which, in fact, applies to almost all the coaching situations that I find myself in.

Everything I do is essentially performance-aimed. I use coaching as a means of getting my staff to a level where I can delegate work to them that I would otherwise have to do myself. I see the time I spend coaching very much as an investment, the dividend from which is the far greater time I save myself through delegation.

Nursing is a profession where learning is a continuing and fundamental part of the job. Sally Bassett, a former Assistant Director of Nursing at the Hillingdon NHS Trust, explains:

A large part of my daily work could be called coaching, although we use the terms teaching and role modelling. But even a newly qualified staff nurse has to be able to coach student nurses, and clearly a 'hands-on' role is required initially when the penalty for a mistake can be unnecessary pain or worse for a patient. In my own case, I have to keep up-to-date with new developments and, while I would expect some 'hands-on' coaching during a demonstration of any new technique, I respond much better to a 'hands-off' approach as I put things into practice.

Garnet Marshall, was director of instructor training at the British School of Motoring and he commented:

Training at BSM is going through a total change of ethos. We think that coaching is a better way of learning rather than the old-fashioned autocratic way of standing up in front of people. We're aiming for a situation where everyone is coached in a way that encourages them to find things out for themselves. I don't want to be in the business of force-feeding people knowledge. In order to create the right environment for people to learn, the trainer must become a facilitator and a coach.

Terry, a BSM driving instructor in Brighton, clearly recognized the 'hands-on' to 'hands-off' coaching spectrum in his job. He has to take a complete beginner who may never have sat behind a wheel before through a test to become a qualified, competent, road safe driver. He reports:

> The first few lessons are really just instruction rather than coaching in its fullest sense. But about halfway through the series of lessons, the learner has been taught or shown everything they need to know. From then on, it's a matter of practising and perfecting. This is where I suppose it becomes more 'hands-off' and in my case feet-off as well. Believe me, I wouldn't be alive now if I didn't have dual controls!
>
> At this stage, I just try and let them drive without interfering. If they make a mistake, I'll tell them and then get them to try and work out what it was and why it happened. If it's a major mistake, then we'll pull over and analyse what went wrong.

Coaching and Learning

Bridget Kearns is Head of Training and Development at First Choice Holidays and has a clear view of the connection between workplace coaching and learning. She claims:

> My team operates on a number of principles. We believe that people need to remember how they learnt as babies. Take learning to walk for example. Most people:
> - did not read it in a book;
> - were self-motivated;
> - failed hundreds of times;
> - found their own way;
> - received oodles of encouragement;
> - every little improvement was celebrated;
> - and no one said 'this is not for you'.
>
> But while we try to ensure that our training courses are supportive, challenging and fun, we also operate the 'before and after' principle. This tells us that what happens during the course itself is relatively unimportant. It's the motivation achieved before the course starts and the sustained effort to apply the messages after the course finishes that are crucially important. And that is why we place so much importance on the role of the manager as coach. The effectiveness of the learning depends on their effectiveness as a coach.

Charlotte Park is Head of Training and Development at Manchester-based engineering components distributor BSL Ltd. She also believes that managers as coaches are a vital link in the learning and development processes:

> Ongoing coaching to develop skills and knowledge is a vital tool for every manager in business today. Releasing staff to attend training courses is becoming increasingly difficult as operations become ever more 'lean and mean' in human resource terms, and one-off events rarely induce the behavioural changes hoped for and therefore prove ineffective in the long term.
>
> Coaching is particularly useful for developing senior managers, especially those who don't always recognize their own weaknesses and, in true British "Macho Management" tradition, often feel uncomfortable actually admitting that they need any development. By setting up ongoing internal peer group coaching and mentoring sessions, ensuring complete confidentiality, senior managers feel able to explore ideas, develop different solutions and accept constructive feedback in a non-threatening way about real life work issues and problems that they are currently facing. In my experience, not only do both parties gain a lot from it, it is also an excellent way to encourage them to make time for conscious development activity, something that would never normally be included in their list of day-to-day priorities.

Managing as a Coach

Coaching Olympic performers to reach even higher standards is a very sophisticated activity. The coach, who is often not at the same performance level as the performer, has to recognize that the performer has total control over performance. The Olympic coach operates in a hands-off style and focuses largely on the mental attitude of the performer rather than their basic skills and techniques. Coaches of top performing teams and of stars in the performing arts have to follow this pattern, too. The same approach to transferring control, as we have seen, applies in the workplace. This transfer of control is illustrated in the following diagram.

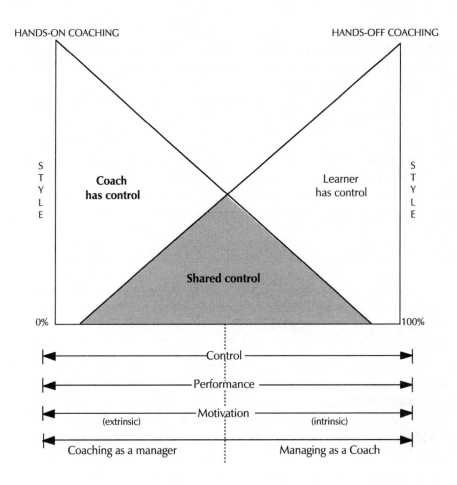

Figure 3.2 *Coaching Management Styles Continuum*

Many managers find it difficult to move quickly along the coaching styles continuum towards a hands-off position. Partly, this is because some managers are locked into a traditional hierarchical command and control management style and are ill-suited and personally uncomfortable with changing style.

Sometimes, too, the culture of their organization and the structure of the jobs that have to be done forces them towards a hands-on style. For instance, in a situation of a simple, repetitive task-oriented department with a high turnover of staff or a heavy reliance on temporary or short-contract people, a coach may be constantly forced into situations where hands-on is the only appropriate style to adopt. Similarly, in situations of great urgency, a fire alarm for instance, there is no time for a period of reflective questioning!

It is also true that where managers are held closely accountable for immediate results with severe penalties for failure, it is difficult for them to take the risk involved in letting go of control and trusting the performer to take responsibility for improving performance. This is a very real problem for many managers, and has been made worse with the increases in workload and stress that has resulted from many experiments with re-engineering, the impact of new technology and mergers.

These pressures help to explain why many coaches and learners are probably operating at around 25–30 per cent along the continuum towards a hands-off style. There has been a lot of talk about sharing control and empowerment, but often there is a real and understandable reluctance to put it into practice.

Of course, there is a fundamental contradiction in this reluctance to change style. Experience shows that higher levels of performance from individuals and teams are more often achieved when people are given greater control and responsibility. So the desire and pressure for ever higher performance standards are often, in practice, frustrated by a reluctance to risk releasing control. This frustration is likely to contribute to the increased stress levels for managers.

For organizations wishing to develop the necessary 'positive learning culture', there is no alternative but for managers to move rapidly down the coaching style continuum toward the hands-off position. This implies a change in management style away from 'coaching as a manager' towards 'managing as a coach'.

Coaching Techniques

Among the most common situations that a coach can face are:

- coaching an inexperienced learner or helping to develop a new skill;

- finding time to help someone to sort out a problem when the coach is under pressure from a heavy workload;

- coaching an experienced and able learner who has the time and motivation to improve their performance.

For each of these situations different coaching techniques can be employed. We'll look at each of them in turn.

Coaching Inexperienced Learners

One technique that has been found most helpful in these situations is called the 'Practice Spiral' (once again, please remember that this is a model, not a set of instructions to be used in any and every situation).

The Practice Spiral starts with an initial explanation and demonstration stage. This is followed by a stage for reflecting on the learning achieved during the initial stage. Then comes a reviewing stage that focuses on drawing specific conclusions about how much progress has been made towards achieving the eventual goal. The final stage involves planning to practise again. This, of course, leads to another new experience, but this time at a slightly higher level of performance.

The whole process begins again and continues to spiral towards higher and higher levels of performance after each new practice session. The process is shown in Figure 3.3 on page 58.

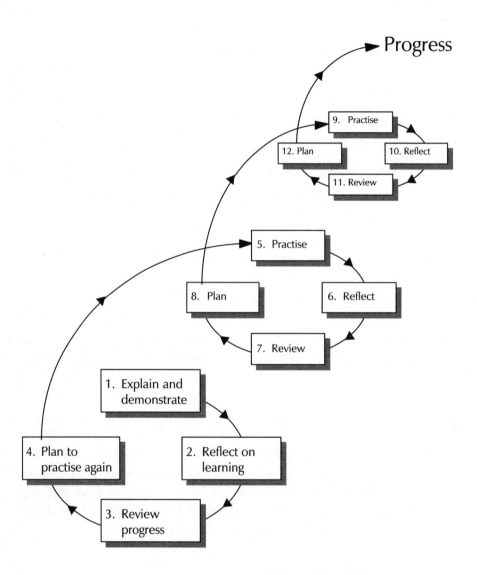

Figure 3.3 *A Practice Spiral*

There are a number of key points for the coach to follow at each stage of the spiral.

Stage 1   Explain and Demonstrate

At this stage the coach should:

- summarize what is about to be explained and demonstrated;

- emphasize why it is important;

- outline how it is going to be done;

- explain and demonstrate, following a logical sequence;

- summarize, re-emphasizing why it is important;

- allow time for questions, clarifications and feedback to check understanding.

Stage 2   Reflect on the Learning

This stage should be deliberately timed. Often, simply allowing a few minutes private thought, note taking or handling of a piece of new equipment is all that is required.

Stage 3   Review Progress

At this stage, the coach needs to remind the learner of the ultimate goal of the learning programme and to encourage them to articulate the progress they feel they have made so far. Skilful questioning can help learners to identify any barriers to learning they are experiencing, as well as enabling them to clarify any areas of misunderstanding which may have arisen.

Stage 4   Plan to Practise Again

Opportunities to practise what has been learnt are crucial to ensure that the required competence standards are achieved. The coach should ensure three types of practice sessions:

- 'risk-free' opportunities: where mistakes can easily be made and remedial action taken with no damage done or blame expressed;

- 'close-observation' opportunities: where learners can practise in real life situations with the coach in close attendance to be able to intervene to help to correct any faults and to build confidence with constructive feedback and praise;

- 'spot-check' opportunities: where the learner is free to operate in a real life situation but with the knowledge that there will be occasional spot-checks by the coach to offer feedback and motivation.

As learners progress up the spiral, the type of practice session the coach will agree with the learner will obviously move from risk-free to spot-check. Note that although the spiral starts with a totally hands-on style, the coach moves steadily down the styles continuum towards a hands-off position.

The 'Skills Framework' Technique

The 'Spiral' technique works well when the inexperienced learner has to acquire a mechanical skill or has to master a new operating process. But when (what is termed) a 'soft skill', like presentation or influencing, has to be learnt or when a combination of process and soft skills, like interviewing skills and techniques, is required, it is more helpful to use a 'framework' technique.

This requires the coach to have a clear competency framework of the identified learning need on which to focus the coaching programme. As an example, we can choose the need to develop 'Appraisal Interviewing Skills and Techniques'. In which case the competency framework on pages 61–62 could have been developed.

Appraisal Interview Skills Framework		
Please tick appropriate column:	YES	NEEDS HELP
Process knowledge The learner understands:		
1.1　The purpose, benefits and limitations of appraisals		
1.2　The organisation's appraisal process:		
• principles		
• practices		
• paperwork		
Process skills and techniques The learner can:		
2.1　Collate and evaluate performance measures (before the appraisal)		
2.2　Prepare for the appraisal (in the weeks before)		
2.3　Brief the team member to prepare themselves		
2.4　Prepare for the appraisal (on the day)		
2.5　Follow a clear structure for the interview		
2.6　Provide feedback on performance during the interview		
2.7　Set objectives during the interview		
2.8　End an appraisal appropriately		

	Please tick appropriate column:	YES	NEEDS HELP
2.9	Help team members who have performance problems		
2.10	Provide ongoing support to achieve results		

Personal skills, style and attitudes

The learner can:

3.1	Communicate effectively during the appraisal		
3.2	Resolve conflicts during appraisals		
3.3	Display a positive attitude towards personal development throughout the appraisal process		

Figure 3.4 *Appraisal Interview Skills Framework*

This framework is a general checklist, which is backed up by a more detailed set of checklists, and now provides both the learner and the coach with an opportunity for a rigorous self-assessment of exactly what the outcome of the learning programme should be. Those areas that the learner already understands and in which they can perform confidently can be ticked off, allowing the coach to focus on those issues that need detailed attention. The coach now follows the normal coaching process model to achieve the required results.

This technique has the benefit of clearly showing that different aspects of the skills and techniques of the development programme will require different learning opportunities to be taken. Some will involve individual study, others observation and practice. While it may be an advantage for the coach to be a skilled interviewer, it is not absolutely necessary. The framework provides the coach with a clear overall appreciation of the desired outcomes and, if necessary, the learner can be given access to alternative and more detailed expertise.

One coach who has used the 'framework' technique to develop customer service telephone effectiveness, which also combine soft and process skills, is Elizabeth Harris, Managing Director of Groom House Training and Development. She comments:

> I am involved in three different development situations. I coach my staff to manage their own learning and performance improvements; I coach-mentor a client to achieve a qualification and I also coach others to develop specific customer service skills.
>
> Each situation calls for a different approach, and I find that a competency framework approach produces the best results when I am helping to improve performance in a specific skill area. It combines a rigorous analysis of the behaviour and performances that are required with an easy-to-use observation and self-assessment checklist. It also helps to ensure consistency of performance, providing all the coaches have a common understanding of the framework before they start coaching.
>
> Remember, that in call centre situations, we may be talking 100 coaches each aiming for the same quality of performance and so consistency is important. To achieve this, there needs to be not just a common understanding of the competences, but for fairness as well. There is therefore a need for regular meetings in which the group of coaches run check assessments to test for fairness and consistency.

One approach we use is to listen to recordings of customer interactions and then independently complete the checklist. Each decides the coaching priorities and discusses them with the rest of the group. If we are doing the job properly, we should all be agreeing on the priority areas for both improvement and reinforcement. We also run role-plays of the coaching meeting to ensure that feedback is given in a constructive way.

Elizabeth is a firm believer that coaching can be seen as the 'glue that makes training stick', particularly when the objective of the intervention is to improve something like customer service effectiveness over the telephone. As she points out:

In these situations the customer service representatives usually need a combination of product knowledge, technical dexterity to operate a computer programme and personal skills. Knowledge can often best be imparted in a training context, but technical and personal skills require continual practice in real life situations. Thus a combination of training and coaching will produce the best results. Organizations that try to save short-term costs by limiting the development to a training course alone usually find that it is an expensive mistake.

We then sometimes find ourselves in a situation where coaching to improve performance is seen as a 'punishment'. The truth is more likely to be either:

- lack of the basic knowledge of how to do it;
- misunderstanding the competences or objectives;
- seeing no reward for doing the job;
- factors outside the control of the individual;
- being unaware of a performance problem.

As coaches, we have to be very careful to identify the root cause of the performance difficulty and work very hard to create the motivation to change behaviour. If the initial development programme had combined training with adequate coaching follow-up, these sorts of difficulties could have been avoided.

The '3–D' Technique

Even when an organization has followed the appropriate learning methodologies to develop its people, operational problems still arise. For example, sometimes people ask for help at inconvenient times for the coach. Most managers are under increasing time pressures and may genuinely find it difficult to reorganize their priorities to meet the immediate needs of a member of their team. Experience has shown that coaches who can cope with these situations are highly regarded by their colleagues and team members.

Successful coaches often express the belief that time spent in coaching to help with immediate problems is repaid many times over through the improvements in performance and higher levels of motivation.

The essence of handling these pressurized coaching sessions is to focus as rapidly as possible on potential solutions that the other person can recognize and take personal responsibility for implementing. The '3–D' technique is one that has been found helpful for these situations. It is based on recognizing a three-dimensional analysis as illustrated in Figure 3.5 on page 66.

To use this technique, a coach simply needs a blank sheet of paper or a flip chart. The learner is asked to quickly define the problem in a single sentence. Careful questioning and using the 3–D analysis technique enable the coach and the learner to quickly identify three elements of the problem under each of three headings:

- *the situation*, eg timescales, lack of resources, geography;

- *people involved*, eg unhappy customer, impatient boss, unreliable supplier;

- *you*, eg lack of technical knowledge, conflicting priorities, the learner's general attitude.

With these three dimensions, or aspects, of the problem identified, it is usually relatively easy to identify several options to choose from – even if most of them require actions related solely to the learner themself!

The final stage is to choose the 'best-fit' option to actually implement.

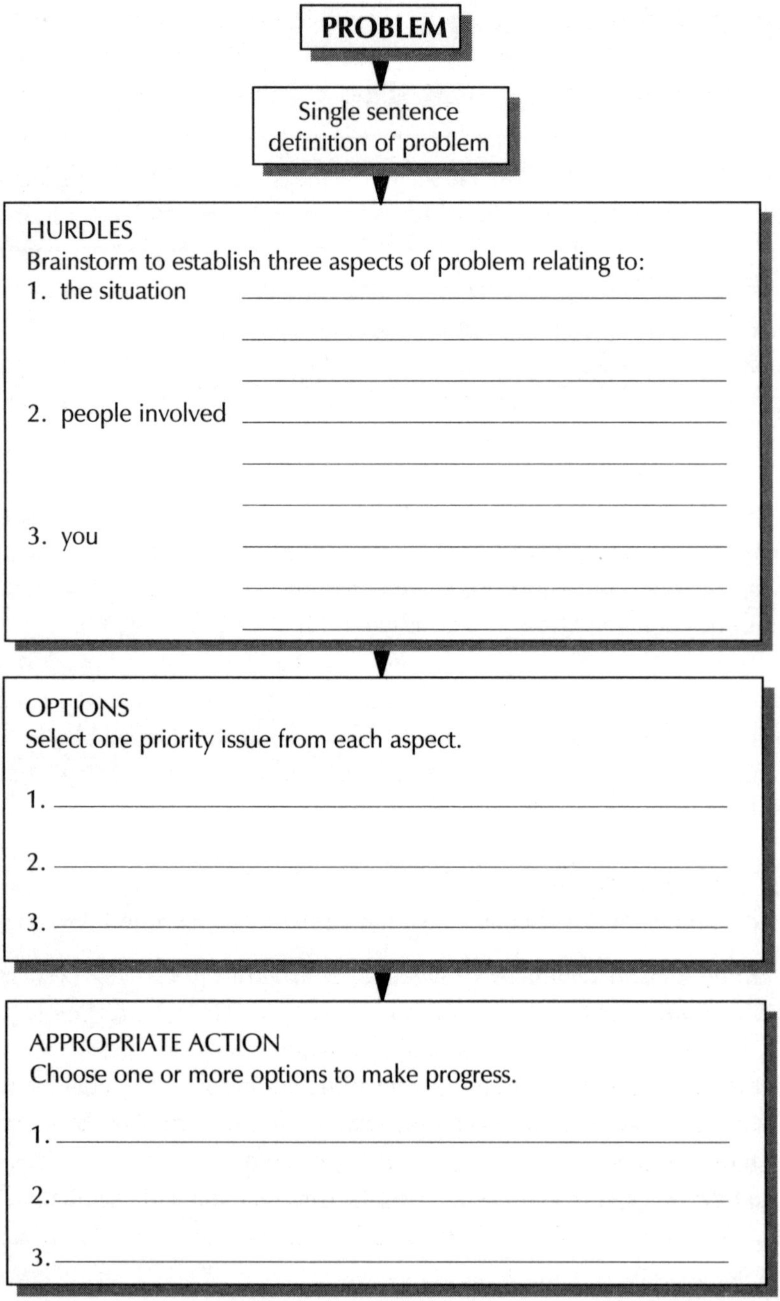

PROBLEM

Single sentence
definition of problem

HURDLES
Brainstorm to establish three aspects of problem relating to:
1. the situation   _____

_____

_____

2. people involved _____

_____

_____

3. you   _____

_____

_____

OPTIONS
Select one priority issue from each aspect.

1. _____

2. _____

3. _____

APPROPRIATE ACTION
Choose one or more options to make progress.

1. _____

2. _____

3. _____

Figure 3.5 *The '3-D' Technique*

Following this structured technique, it is possible to focus rapidly on potential actions. By relying almost entirely on questioning, the coach can help people to articulate most of the issues and options themselves. The coach will have enabled the learner to focus more clearly and leave the responsibility for taking final decisions with them. With practice, this technique can work in 10–15 minutes.

It is also possible to use the 3–D technique to coach yourself through a problem. You can try it for yourself now:

1. Define a current problem in a single sentence.

2. List three general issues relating to the problem *situation*.

3. List three issues relating to the *people* involved.

4. List three issues that relate specifically to *you* and the problem.

5. Choose one issue from each of your three lists of three issues.

6. Now identify one or more options that are most likely to make progress in solving the problem.

It may seem quite simple, but it works. The technique works best when the coach relies entirely on questioning to encourage the learner to work through the process.

The GROW Technique

The GROW technique has its origins in sports coaches who have been influenced by Tim Gallwey's book *The Inner Game of Tennis* (1974). The technique relies heavily on using skilful questions and following a clear structure.

First, the questions focus on the 'Goal' the learner wants to achieve in the immediate coaching session. Next, the focus is on the total 'Reality' in which the learner is operating. This is followed by questioning the practical 'Options' that the learner might choose, to achieve the goal that they have set themselves. Finally, the focus is on the 'Will 'to actually take specific action to implement one or more of the options previously chosen.

So the easy way to remember the structure is to use the mnemonic which summarizes the GROW technique as:

- establish the **G**oal;

- examine the **R**eality;

- consider all **O**ptions;

- confirm the **W**ill to act.

GROW is a powerful technique when you are coaching learners who already have a basic knowledge, expertise and enthusiasm for the issue involved. This is generally true in a sports context, but is often not the case in work situations. With inexperienced learners – or coaches for that matter – the GROW technique is, in our experience, often too time consuming and sophisticated for practical day-to-day work-based coaching situations.

However, where the coach has the time, patience and skills, the GROW technique is an excellent coaching technique for the 'hands-off' coaching style with a proven record of success. The key skills are effective questioning and systematically following the GROW structure during the coaching session. It is often an interactive process and cannot easily be rushed. The end result of coaching with GROW can be a highly-focused and motivated learner. We discuss the types of questions that are appropriate to use with this technique in Chapter 8.

Coaching for Successful Team Performance

A team can be defined as 'two or more people working together to achieve results'. In practice, a coach can usually expect to be effective with teams of about 12 to 15 people. Beyond that size, more than one coach is often required.

A particularly successful sports coach is David Whitaker, who has translated his success with the British Hockey team in the Seoul Olympics into effective business coaching. His experience is with team coaching. He explains:

> Teams require individual and small-group coaching as well as whole team coaching sessions. The coach knows he is being successful when the players take over the coaching sessions themselves. This allows the coach to 'helicopter' above the team and take an overall view. Interventions become more selective and are expressed in a way that doesn't disturb the ownership of responsibility among the players for

> their own performance. The really effective coach works himself out
> of the job. My team talk before the gold medal final in Seoul was
> simply 'I know that you know what you are going to do – good luck.'

They did and they won (personal communication, 1999). The effectiveness of a team is the sum of the individual members' contributions. Tim Gallwey is credited with articulating the formula:

POTENTIAL – INTERFERENCE = PERFORMANCE

This positions the coach's main task as reducing or removing the 'interferences' that block an individual or team producing their optimum levels of performance. The coach, therefore, has to harmonize individual effort into cohesive team action to achieve the desired performance results. The basic rules of coaching as a process, which require the application of styles, techniques and skills, also apply to team coaching. In addition, however, a team coach needs to understand the fundamentals of team dynamics and the different ways that individuals can contribute to successful team performance.

Comparing successful sporting teams to the world of work can be useful. The foundations of successful sporting teams are built on the coach ensuring:

- that there are the right number of players with the basic skills, experience and knowledge of the rules of the game;

- good matching of players to positions and players who know what is expected of them individually and as a team;

- regular training and practice on good, well-maintained equipment;

- good communication of strategy and tactics;

- regular reviews on performance, with encouraging and supportive feedback;

- that mistakes are treated as learning opportunities, not occasions for blame and punishment.

This combination of technical expertise, development opportunities and attitudes is equally true of work as well as of play.

Helicopter vs Seagulls

Team coaching requires the coach to operate in one-to-one situations as well as in small and large groups. The GROW technique has proved successful in providing a structure to handle this wide variety of situations, although the coach needs to develop a special expertise to handle a group discussion using the GROW technique.

A successful team coach also needs to develop a 'helicopter' quality. This is the ability to rise above day-to-day events and pressures and take an overview of what is actually happening or likely to happen. It is rather like hovering in an aerial position so that 'the wood can be seen from the trees'.

Taking this more detached and objective view allows the coach to swoop down to help to correct individual problems, but also quietly to resume a more detached strategic and tactical view and allowing the team the maximum control of immediate performance.

The 'helicopter' quality is quite different from a 'seagull' quality. A seagull coach is best described as someone who flies in, circles around, makes a lot of noise, swoops down and craps on a few people and quickly flies off again!

Assessing Your Coaching Competence

To help you to summarize the messages of this chapter, you may care to complete the following self-assessment exercise to help you to establish your current levels of competence as a coach. Often our own perceptions are more critical than others, but we may also be unaware of some aspects of our behaviour. Self-assessment is a powerful technique for raising awareness and providing an agenda for open dialogue with your colleagues and your coach.

Performance Criteria

Assessment Guidelines

There are three commonsense levels of assessment:

Good   which is above standard
OK   which is acceptable
Needs help   which is self-explanatory and is the information on
                  which to base a PDP

Stage 1: Analyse for Awareness

You accurately assess the current standards of
performance of the learner as an individual and as a
team player.

☐ Good
☐ OK
☐ Needs help

You accurately identify the future performance
goals of the learner, and gain positive agreement to
attain them.

☐ Good
☐ OK
☐ Needs help

Stage 2: Plan for Responsibility

You agree learning opportunities most suited to the learning style preferences of the learner.	☐ Good ☐ OK ☐ Needs help
Your skills coaching plan is based on the correct sequence of the components of the skill.	☐ Good ☐ OK ☐ Needs help
You agree methods of regularly monitoring performance and choosing opportunities for applying the learning.	☐ Good ☐ OK ☐ Needs help
You maximise the scope for the learner to manage their own development and take responsibility for meeting their goals.	☐ Good ☐ OK ☐ Needs help
You organize the appropriate time and space for the learner to practise skills and gain experience in a structured way.	☐ Good ☐ OK ☐ Needs help
You agree and/or facilitate the appropriate level of support for the learner.	☐ Good ☐ OK ☐ Needs help

Stage 3: Implement for Action		
You adjust your coaching style and technique to take account of the learner's progress and level of performance.	☐	Good
	☐	OK
	☐	Needs help
You explain and demonstrate skills and techniques using an appropriate manner and pace.	☐	Good
	☐	OK
	☐	Needs help
You ensure sufficient opportunities for practice, feedback and discussion to occur.	☐	Good
	☐	OK
	☐	Needs help
You ensure that adequate communication occurs with other people invovled in the development process.	☐	Good
	☐	OK
	☐	Needs help

Stage 4: Evaluate for Success		
You regularly evaluate the achievement of goals and standards and explore any factors inhibiting the learning.	☐	Good
	☐	OK
	☐	Needs help
You provide encouragement and support to the learner to apply their learning.	☐	Good
	☐	OK
	☐	Needs help
You motivate the learner to set new development goals and agree the ongoing support they need.	☐	Good
	☐	OK
	☐	Needs help
You analyse the learner's preferred learning style and identify any barriers to learning.	☐	Good
	☐	OK
	☐	Needs help
The techniques you use encourage the learner to develop an all-round awareness of themselves and their working environment.	☐	Good
	☐	OK
	☐	Needs help

Figure 3.6 *Assessment of competence*

Chapter 4

Mentoring: Where Theory and Practice Collide

In Chapter 1, we established that there is no consensus yet on terminology in the field of coaching and mentoring and that current terms and definitions may continue to change as the 'revolution in thinking' continues. We have also noted that theoretical models are useful only if they are used to help us to understand new ideas or concepts, and to design models that suit our own specific situations. Applications and experiences of coaching and mentoring are likely to be different in different international and cultural contexts and we are all still learning. In this chapter, we shall see just how strongly traditional theory and practice of mentoring collide and create the need for new thinking and terminology.

While mentoring is basically a one-to-one activity, it can happen in many different contexts or environments:

- Business-to-business, where the main thrust is on economic regeneration and where a mentor from a large organization works with one from a small or medium-sized enterprise.

- Business-to-enterprise, where, for example a Trust like the Prince's Youth Business Trust has mentors to guide young 'starters' in business who have received grants from them.

- The Government's Fair Deal programme, similar to business-to-enterprise, but where the learner might have special needs in gaining access to employment.

- Special needs and community projects, where the mentoring is more personal and designed for individual needs and where matching the mentor and learner may be critical.

- Business-to-education, where business people volunteer to work with headteachers, teachers and students.

- Graduate or undergraduate mentoring, where more experienced people help to guide or counsel students through different stages of their studies.

Corporate mentoring roles are often designed to support specific groups:

- new recruits;

- graduate trainees;

- women;

- ethnic minorities;

- disabled or disadvantaged individuals;

- individuals facing a career change, redundancy or pre-retirement;

- people with a specific desire and motivation to manage their own learning and development.

It is hardly surprising that no single definition or model uniformly fits all these different contexts. We need to try to understand both the differences and the similarities.

Definitions of Mentoring

Mentor was the name of a character from Greek mythology who was a wise and trusted adviser or counsellor. The word has, until recently, kept that meaning. It is a word that is often used by politicians, sports people, actors and other performers to describe the person whom they chose as a role model or someone who had a significant early influence on their professional careers.

We can probably all identify people who have been significant in our development. Eric Parsloe can identify an uncle, a friend who was successful in business, and a non-executive chairman who have all played a mentoring role for him. They played this role at different times in differing degrees and for different lengths of time. Two of them he selected himself rather unconsciously, the other one was politely imposed on him. All three helped him considerably, but at no time did they use the term 'mentor'; it just happened. His experience, we suspect, mirrors many others and left to itself, mentoring would have gone on in this way, as it has for hundreds of years.

Times have changed, however. Mentoring has become a business and policy makers' buzzword. Imported in its new form from the United States in the late 1980s, it was initially viewed somewhat suspiciously in the UK as another 'flavour of the month'. Still worse, its use as a vocational verb – 'to mentor' – was resented by some traditionalists as another example of the 'Americanization' of the English language.

As with coaching, there are almost as many definitions of mentoring as there are individual coaches, mentors or tutors. The terms are often used interchangeably. The following definitions give an indication of the wide variety of interpretations of mentoring in the workplace, education and the community:

- One of the earliest British writers to attempt a definition was David Megginson (1979) who wrote:

  > Mentoring is an essential aid to staff development ... which calls for a perspective that looks for future possibilities. This requires a level of trust missing from the judgemental line management relationship where discipline has to be maintained and performance assessed.

- A report published in 1989 by the then Council for National Academic Awards and the Government Training Agency discussed mentoring in these terms:

There are many views and definitions of the role of mentor, but all include verbs like support, guide, facilitate, etc. Important aspects are to do with listening, questioning and enabling, as distinct from telling, directing and restricting. Mentors are crucial to good management development since they can exert great influence in developing attitudes and encouraging good managerial practice. ...high quality mentoring is concerned with competence, experience and clear role-definition, but it also crucially depends upon the right balance of personal qualities.

● In 1991, David Clutterbuck wrote in his book *Everyone Needs a Mentor*:

A mentor is a more experienced individual willing to share their knowledge with someone less experienced in a relationship of mutual trust. A mixture of parent and peer, the mentor's primary function is to be a transitional figure in an individual's development.

Mentoring includes coaching, facilitating, counselling and networking. It is not necessary to dazzle the protégé with knowledge and experience. The mentor just has to provide encouragement by sharing his enthusiasm for his job.

● There have been other definitions along the way, including:

In the modern business context, mentoring is always at least one stage removed (from direct line management responsibility), and is concerned with the longer-term acquisition and application of skills in a developing career by a form of advising and counselling.
(Parsloe, E, *Coaching, Mentoring and Assessing*, 1992)

Mentors are people who, through their action and work, help others to achieve their potential.
(Shea, G F, *Mentoring: a guide to the basics*, 1992)

Whether we label it coaching, advising, counselling or mentoring, if done well its effectiveness will depend in large measure on the manager's belief about human potential.
(Whitmore, J, *Coaching for Performance*, 1997)

Mentoring is a role which includes coaching, but also embraces broader counselling and support, such as career counselling, privileged access to information, etc.
(Landsberg, M, *The Tao of Coaching*, 1996)

Behind every successful person, there is one elementary truth: somewhere, somehow, someone cared about their growth and development. This person was their mentor.'
(Kaye, B L, *Up is Not the Only Way*)

- In 1998, Clutterbuck, writing in *Learning Alliances – Tapping into Talent*, had developed his thinking and now described mentoring as an integrating role and wrote:

    Mentoring is one of the most powerful developmental approaches available to individuals and organizations. Certainly the spread of planned mentoring programmes, first in the USA, then in Europe and Asia-Pacific, has been rapid.

    Much of the widespread confusion about what is and what is not mentoring comes from the fact that there are two distinct schools of thought. The traditional, North American concept of mentoring is embodied by someone older and more powerful, who expects loyalty in return for advice, guidance and a helping hand. In this person-ification, the mentor may be the person's line manager. The term protégé is typically used to describe the relationship, which places relatively little emphasis on learning (by either party) and a lot on assistance with making the right career moves.

    By contrast, the European concept of mentoring assumes that the mentor has more experience rather than more power. Indeed, a characteristic of an effective mentoring relationship is the 'parking' of any power differences so that the two can deal as equals. As a result, European mentors are almost always off-line, not least because it is difficult to be very open to someone who has the power to influence your pay, status and general well-being. The purpose of the relationship is primarily learning or development, although a result of learning may well be better career management by the mentee.

- The European Mentoring Centre, which reflects a growing consensus (non-US) view, now has a catch-all definition of mentoring as:

    Off-line help by one person to another in making significant transitions in knowledge, work or thinking.

Faced with this rather bewildering set of descriptions and language, it must be tempting for people wanting to establish a mentoring programme to conclude that mentoring in the work or community context can mean anything you like to describe it as.

In a sense, this should not surprise us. What we are involved in is a 'revolution in thinking' about education, training and development with new practices and processes being articulated and applied. It will take time for clear definitions and use of terminology to become established.

Mentoring Defined (a Millennium Attempt)

Our research over recent years into mentoring as a management and community activity in the UK suggests that it may be most helpful to distinguish between the noun, the adjective and the verb in seeking clearer definitions.

Asking 'What is a mentor?' (noun) leads us to recognize three broad primary types (adjective plus noun), albeit with different titles than we suggested in 1990. Within each primary type of mentoring, there are a number of subsidiary mentoring roles (nouns) each of which may also need an adjective to describe it accurately, for instance:

> A community mentor (a primary type)
>
> includes
>
> both a 'guidance provider' and a 'good parent' (as different roles that the community mentor can play).

The three broad primary types of mentor are:

- the **'corporate mentor'** who acts as a guide, adviser, and counsellor at various stages in someone's career from induction through formal development to a senior management position and possibly into retirement;

- the **'qualification mentor'** who is required by a professional association or government-sponsored agency to be appointed to guide a candidate through their programme of study, leading to a professional qualification or a National Vocational Qualification (NVQ);

- the **'community mentor'** who acts as a friend, expert adviser or counsellor to individuals in a wide range of situations where the individual may be disadvantaged or in an actual or potentially distressful position.

Examples of these three types of mentor can, of course, be found in many organizations, sometimes all three simultaneously in a single large organization. In this chapter, we will discuss both the 'corporate' and 'qualification' mentor. The 'community' mentor is such an important recent development that we deal with it separately in Chapter 5.

Towards a Definition

Asking 'What is mentoring?' leads us to definitions that describe the activities that mentors actually 'do'. Given that the behaviour of mentors is, or we believe *should be*, determined by the specific context in which they are working in, we believe that this question is best answered by first describing mentoring primarily as:

> a process that supports and encourages learning to happen.

This then allows us to further describe mentoring, as with coaching, in terms of role, style, techniques, skills and quality of the relationship.

The terms mentoring and coaching are clearly used to describe a wide variety of activities. However, lazy use of words allows them to mean different things to different people within the same organization or community context, which is, at best, unnecessarily confusing and, at worst, dangerously misleading. The need for clarity is important and should be the first task in any exercise to introduce a mentoring or coaching programme or scheme. We suggest that the following definition helps to make a clearer distinction between 'coaching' and 'mentoring':

> The distinction between coaching and mentoring is one of contextual roles, responsibilities and relationships as both are processes that enable or support and encourage learning to happen.
> A 'corporate mentor' is rarely a learner's line manager. A 'qualification mentor' is almost always more experienced and qualified themselves. A 'community mentor' can be anyone who has the ability and willingness to help.
> All mentors seek to develop a special relationship as close as possible to the traditional concept of a trusted advisor and counsellor. They can be more interested in improvements in performance and behaviour over a longer time scale, possibly a whole career, than is

the case with the necessary 'immediate results focus' of a line manager, qualification supervisor or personal skills coach.

This broad definition aims to make a distinction between coaching and mentoring for organizations with a typical line management structure. In small or voluntary organizations these distinctions may not easily apply. In some creative businesses with no real line management structure, for instance, coaching may be defined as a responsibility for everyone in the organization. In these cases, mentoring may then be an additional role for only the top management team with the responsibility to encourage, support and agree an individual's Personal Development Plan. However, remember the caveat that 'mentoring is always defined specifically by the context of the employing organization'.

So, while there are almost as many definitions of mentoring as there are mentoring programmes, each of them valid in their own context, it is useful to define mentoring as a *process which supports learning and development, and thus performance improvements, either for an individual, team or business*. Mentoring is also usefully understood as a special kind of relationship where objectivity, credibility, honesty, trustworthiness and confidentiality are critical.

When all the theory is stripped away, however, mentoring is still simply about a regular one-to-one meeting to support the learner in their desire to improve their personal situation or their business life.

Mentoring as a Process

Mentoring, like coaching, is a process. However, while coaching is an enabling and helping process, mentoring is essentially a supportive process. It would be convenient if the mentoring process was as uniform as the coaching process. Unfortunately this is not the case, as the 'community mentoring' process has some important differences from the 'corporate' and 'qualification' processes. Let us first describe the corporate and qualification processes.

Corporate and Qualification Mentoring Processes

The words used to describe each stage of the process for both these roles reflect the distinctions between them and the community mentor process. The key process stages are:

Stage 1   **Confirm the Personal Development Plan (PDP);**

Stage 2   **Encourage self-management of learning;**

Stage 3   **Provide support during the PDP process;**

Stage 4   **Assist in the evaluation of success.**

The use of these words also reflects the different roles, responsibilities and accountabilities of a mentor from that of a coach. Mentors, in the workplace, are rarely a learner's direct line manager whereas a coach usually is. The mentoring process can be illustrated graphically, as in Figure 4.1:

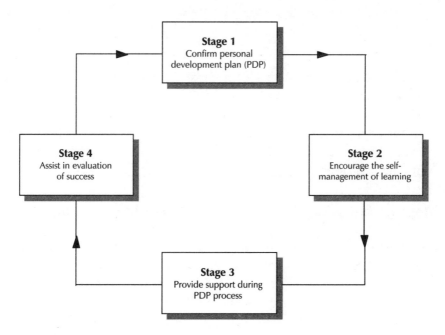

Figure 4.1 *The Mentoring Process*

Let's now focus on some of the key tasks of a mentor during each stage of the process.

Stage 1 Confirm the Personal Development Plan

- Final responsibility for the Personal Development Plan lies with the learner and their '(manager) coach'. A mentor may be involved at any stage during the preparation of the PDP, but their role is simply to help to confirm by providing guidance, access to information and acting as a 'sounding-board'. The mentor has no direct responsibility or accountability for the learner's performance although, in the qualification context, they are often required to follow set guidelines.

- The mentor has to prepare for their role by analysing, identifying and anticipating the likely needs that the learner will have in achieving their learning and development goals. The mentor will need to be sensitive to all the circumstances within which the learner is operating, including their personal beliefs, capabilities, aspirations and learning style preferences.

- The mentor needs to encourage the development of self-awareness in the learner by showing how self-assessment and honest open questioning can help to achieve this.

- One of the key areas where a mentor may help is by checking that all the learning and development goals meet the SMART criteria. (Specific, Measurable, Achieveable, Relevant and Timescaled). The mentor can also usefully draw attention to the need to set goals with short and realistic time scales. Even a long qualification programme is more successfully tackled in short manageable stages.

Stage 2 Encourage the Self-management of Learning

- One of the characteristics of a good PDP is the extent to which it allows for self-management of the process. However, not all learners will have sufficient experience to manage the implementation of the PDP. The mentor's greater experience should allow them, by asking probing questions, to encourage the learner to think ahead and anticipate some of the administrative aspects of implementing the PDP.

- The mentor can also provide a useful service by giving clear explanations and reminders at the appropriate moment of the range of support options that may be available.

- One of the most critical aspects of the mentoring role is to ensure that the day-to-day working relationship between the learner and the line manager is not compromised by the mentor's activities. Learners should be encouraged on all occasions to work out their own solutions to any problem they have with their line manager or other colleagues. A mentor is a 'sounding-board', not a trouble-shooter. Conversations need to be in strict confidence so that a genuine level of trust can exist. Only in the most extreme situations should a mentor intervene directly. Adopting a genuinely objective, confidential and impartial role may not always be easy in practice, but it is essential.

Stage 3   Provide Support during the PDP Implementation Process

- As soon as the PDP starts to be implemented, the mentor needs to be available to provide support. In practical terms, this means agreeing a schedule of meetings as frequently as seems necessary. It is also useful to agree methods for arranging impromptu meetings or contact to deal with any urgent and unforeseen difficulties.

- The way in which the mentor provides guidance and information is critical. Timing, pace and level are obviously important, but the danger of imposing the mentor's natural preferences must be guarded against. Avoiding bias of all kinds and remaining objective, while at the same time fully involved, is not always an easy balance to strike.

- Mentors will sometimes be asked to provide advice and make suggestions. The key here is to ensure that advice and suggestions are given only when requested and not imposed on the learner in an attempt to appear helpful. The mentor is definitely not expected to be the source of all knowledge and information, and they should be quite willing to direct learners to alternative and perhaps more appropriate sources.

- A key role for the mentor is to help learners to deal with mistakes and setbacks which in some line management relationships may result in blame, guilt and feelings of inadequacy. The mentoring relationship should be non-judgemental and 'risk-free'. This allows the mentor to help the learner to treat mistakes and setbacks as real learning opportunities. Properly handled, these situations are often rich learning experiences.

- At all times, the mentor should try to build self-confidence and motivation in the learner, in order to develop a positive attitude and a will to complete the PDP.

Stage 4 Assist in the Evaluation of Success

- There is a distinction between regular monitoring of progress and final evaluation at the end of the PDP. A mentor's role is to encourage the learners to arrange formal evaluations with their line managers or qualification supervisors.

- Helping the learner to prepare for a formal evaluation is a useful mentoring function. Reminding them of the value of self-ssessment and peer-assessment of performance standards is particularly helpful.

- Mentors can use reflective questions to help learners to analyse the causes of any barriers to learning that occur, as well as quantifying the benefits that were gained by themselves and the organization during the PDP process.

- Formal mentoring relationships usually come to an end. Most often this occurs when a learner changes job or with the achievement of a professional or vocational qualification. Ending a relationship is often not easy. Celebrating success and recognizing the mutual benefits gained is important. The mentor should make a special effort to encourage the learner to continue to set new development and career goals. Agreeing to maintain interest and contact in the future is a positive note to end on.

What Happens in Practice?

We have chosen four examples that illustrate the wide variations in the application of mentoring theory and practice. The first relates to the role of 'qualification' mentor the other three relate to 'corporate' mentoring.

Example 1 The 'Qualification' Mentor

The Institute of Chartered Accountants (ICA) has used the concept of mentoring for many years as part of the process of qualifying candidates to full membership of the Institute. They use the word 'counsellor' rather than mentor but the roles are very similar and, like many other instances, also include a role as expert advisor and assessor.

The Institute requires all professional accountancy firms, who are registered members of the Institute, to follow strict guidelines on the training, development and eventual qualification of candidate members of the Institute.

Every authorized training organization has to appoint a 'Member Responsible for Training' who has to already be a qualified member of the Institute themselves. The firm also has to appoint a 'counsellor' and a 'supervisor' (in ICA terms, the counsellor is the mentor and the supervisor, the line manager, is the coach in effect). The ICA roles and responsibilities are clearly laid down as follows:

Counsellor

The training organization must appoint a counsellor for every student under training, ensuring that the number assigned to the person nominated is not so large to inhibit ready access by the student and the proper fulfilment of the role. A ratio of 15 students per counsellor has usually been acceptable, but much will depend on the counsellor's other commitments.

A counsellor should normally be a member of the Institute. If that is not feasible, the counsellor must be a member of the Scottish, or Irish Institute, or of ACCA, CIMA, or CIPFA.

Responsibilities

Working closely with the 'Member Responsible for Training', the counsellor has responsibility for:

A. counselling arrangements, to ensure students have access to counselling at any time;

B. delegation of counselling functions (where appropriate);

C. students' personal and professional development;

D. reviewing students' examination studies and performance;

E. unless undertaken by the Member Responsible for Training, conducting the formal half-yearly reviews of students' progress;

F. confirming to the Member Responsible for Training, that a student is fit to become a member of the Institute;

G. ensuring that any successor is provided with all relevant information about the students to whom he or she is to become counsellor.

Supervisor

The supervisor is the individual in the line management chain to whom the student reports in the first instance whilst preparing for, and undertaking, a particular assignment or task.

The supervisor need not have any formal professional qualifications, but he or she must be someone of the right calibre who has had prior training and/or experience in supervision and who:

A. is technically competent and sufficiently up to date to undertake and supervise the assignment or task;

B. is able to analyse work into the main technical work experience categories;

C. has a working knowledge of the Institute's Guide to Professional Ethics and is able to apply the advice it contains;

D. understands the Institute's recording and progress monitoring system;

E. understands the components of supervision.

In view of the foregoing, it is desirable that the appointment of a supervisor should be endorsed by the Member Responsible for Training.

Responsibilities

The supervisor is responsible for:

A. liaising closely with senior supervisors, managers, counsellors and the Member Responsible for Training in respect of students' work experience, progress and performance;

B. before starting an assignment or task, conducting an oral briefing with the student for the purpose of ensuring that objectives are clear;

C. supervising work experience;

D. conducting an oral review of the work with the student;

E. assessing the student's progress in preparation for the student's half-yearly review.

These are the official guidelines and what happens in practice can vary considerably. In the large firm, KPMG for instance, the ICA guidelines are translated thus as John Bailey (Development Advisor) and Catherine Miller (Manager Responsible for Audit Training) explain:

> KPMG does have a *Member Responsible for Training* who is known as the Exam Training Partner. He is responsible within the organization as the official point of contact for the Institute's education and training system.
>
> There are also *Counselling Partners* who are responsible for monitoring the longer term development of an individual. His or her role is to ensure that the individual's appraisal objectives are set and met through appropriate training and experience. They also ensure that the individual's development is on course to achieve their career ambitions. The Counselling Partner is responsible for reviewing and signing the individual's admission forms to the Institute on behalf of KPMG.

KPMG also assigns *Counselling Managers* to be responsible for meeting individuals every 6 to 12 months to review their performance in the intervening period as well as any training they have received and the experience they have gained. This person is within the line management hierarchy of the appraisee and therefore could be their manager or senior manager.

Assistant managers and managers have day-to-day responsibility for individuals. Before the individual starts an assignment, they will be briefed by an assistant manager or manager. The individual's objectives for the assignment will be jointly agreed. While the work is being completed, the assistant manager or manager will supervise the individual, providing coaching where necessary. They will then review the work and discuss performance. The individual will perform a self-assessment which will then be discussed with the assistant manager or manager. Strengths as well as areas for development are considered and an action plan determined. A written record is maintained.

In addition, KPMG operates a separate *mentoring scheme* for new employees.

When a new graduate joins the firm, they are assigned a mentor to support and guide them through the early years. This person is at least one year more senior to the graduate and so is knowledgeable about KPMG, yet still remembers the pressure of studying for exams. The mentor acts as a buddy and has a confidential relationship with the graduate. They also take on 'a developmental role', coaching and counselling the trainee as necessary on a more informal basis. The guidance provided is based around KPMG's Passport scheme. The 'Passport' sets out the competencies which the firm expects staff to demonstrate as well as providing guidance as to how to develop and demonstrate these competencies.

During the first year of employment, the mentor and mentee meet together on a regular basis, discuss progress and developmental needs as well as any concerns which the individual may have. After the first year, the relationship tends to continue on a more *ad hoc* basis. Mentors are volunteers and the role provides the mentor with the opportunity to develop their own 'people' skills. The aim is that each mentor is assigned to only one mentee so that greater input is provided.

Mentors receive a day of internal training on their role. The emphasis is on the practicalities of the role and centres on the knowledge and tools required by the mentor to develop the mentee. In addition, the course provides a forum for mentors to raise any concerns about their role.

KPMG's approach illustrates how the 'qualification' and 'corporate' mentor's roles overlap with the coaches in some instances. However, in situations where NVQs are operating, it is likely that the roles are far more prescribed and separated. Special training and qualifications are also a requirement for the various advisor, assessor and mentoring roles.

The next three examples all relate to 'corporate' mentoring.

Example 2   The Executive Mentor

Company directors and chief executives have probably always looked for counsel and guidance from outside their organizations on an informal, unpaid basis. The concept of the paid mentor to senior executives, based on a formal agreement, is a more modern and increasingly popular arrangement.

As Clutterbuck and Megginson explain and demonstrate in their book *Mentoring Executives and Directors (1999)*, there are different levels of formality at which executive mentoring takes place – from the formal and paid to the more informal and unpaid. They write:

> There is also an executive mentoring role that falls between the formal and informal where a retiring CEO becomes a mentor to his or her successor.
>
> Executive mentors do much the same as other mentors do, but they need credibility at the highest level of business and often an accompanying knowledge and experience base. Mentoring roles are still that of acting as sounding board, critical friend, listener, advisor, guide. They may also choose to coach on behaviour and/or counsel on how to deal with others' behaviour.

Megginson and Clutterbuck identify three common executive mentoring roles:

- The *executive coach* is usually part of a short-term relationship, based on a clearly defined skills or behavioural issue for the executive concerned.

- The *elder statesman* is typically the senior player who has 'been there, seen it, done it'. Elder statesmen give the benefit of their experience and may act as role models.

- The *reflective mentors* operate at a more holistic level... 'they help executives explore their own issues, build their own insights and self-awareness and develop their own unique ways of handling how they interact with key colleagues and the business. They use current issues to examine recurrent patterns of thinking and behaviour, asking penetrating questions and stimulating the executive to take control of the issues s/he has avoided. They build the executive's confidence through greater self-understanding'.

Executive mentoring is seen by Megginson and Clutterbuck as difficult to do well, as it operates at several different levels – the intellectual, the emotional and the business context.

> The mentor has to be flexible, challenging, rigorous, aware of the executive's needs, ambitions and values, and have a breadth of knowledge about the world of business/work. The success of the relationship between mentor and executive lies also in the latter being prepared to accept the partnership, preparing for the sessions and valuing the opportunity to learn about both their personal and work lives.

Example 3   Mentoring in Sandwell Metropolitan Borough Council IT Division

There were several reasons why the Information Technology Division at Sandwell Metropolitan Borough Council chose to start a mentoring programme, most of which emerged during preparatory work for Investors in People (IIP) reassessment.

The corporate Employee Development Scheme (EDS) was not working particularly well within the Division. It was based on an annual development interview, which tended to result in a list of planned training courses as opposed to 'owned' self-development. Some managers were too keen to please staff while some staff had fixed views on their development wishes. Some plans for the year ahead tended to be unrealistic and failed to materialize therefore leading to a degree of cynicism. The needs of the business also tended to change during the year – IT is very fast moving. Although the EDS scheme was meant to be an overall framework, many development opportunities were being taken up as and when they arose. For example, NVQ programmes offered to all staff at a particular point in time.

By its very nature, working in IT calls for much self-managed learning. Change is constant and it is essential to learn on-the-job in order to keep up to date. Reliance on frequent training courses is neither realistic nor economic. A

Self-Managed Integrated Learning system (SMILE) developed by Wolsey Hall, Oxford was chosen as the 'tool' to replace the existing development scheme. This was welcomed for many reasons: as a means of encouraging ownership of learning; as providing a holistic approach to learning; and as a way of enabling staff to accept that change is constant and that they had to be flexible yet responsive – 'learn how to manage their own career'.

By deciding to use SMILE, the IT Division was in effect endorsing a mentoring programme. As Mark Wheatley, Head of the IT Division explained:

> The main reason for using mentoring was that it was an integral part of the SMILE approach. The process ensures that the learners set their own agenda for the sessions and keep their own records of their action points. The various reflection and self-assessment cycles within SMILE repeatedly bring them back to the learning objectives and creates virtuous circles.

The mentoring programme in the IT Division took place in two phases. Phase One began in July 1998 and was intended to run for six months. It involved a single section of 12 staff . The whole group had a short initial briefing session, and the four most senior members of the team received mentoring each month from an external mentor. As they in turn mentored two other colleagues each, the process cascaded throughout the section.

As the mentors were managers or supervisors from within the same team as their learners, they inevitably acted as both mentors and coaches. However, the emphasis of the programme was firmly on mentoring. The aim was:

> To encourage the learner to do the work themselves and to reflect; for the mentor to act as a mirror. The discipline of the SMILE meeting puts the onus on the learner to use their mentor as a sounding board but to solve their own problems. The mentor's role is to ensure it is the learner's agenda (that is discussed).

Within four months, it was decided to extend the self-managed learning programme, as the advising consultants for IIP were impressed by what it had to offer. Phase Two had a different focus – cross-team mentoring. The impetus for this development was 'to provide a better one-Division approach'. In a Division where there is a potential risk of people being a 'little bit precious about their specialist expertise', there was a need to reinforce co-operation so that customers receive 'joined-up solutions' to meet their needs.

Phase Two began in November 1998 and absorbed Phase One, thus providing an ongoing programme of both 'within-team' and 'cross-team' mentoring. A total of 29 staff (about 40 per cent of the Division) volunteered to participate in this second phase. The existing mentors, who already had two team members as learners, took on a third from outside the team. A couple of learners from Phase One became mentors themselves, and some new mentors were taken from the remaining senior managers who had all volunteered to join the programme. All the mentors had monthly sessions with an external mentor, which enabled them to develop their expertise by role-modelling and discussion.

Phase Two was also originally designed to run for six months, but it very quickly became evident that it was superior to the existing EDS and so it was decided to continue with it. An evaluation after some five months of operation confirmed this. As issues around people's aspirations or performance came up at EDS, they were encouraged (but not coerced) to join the new programme. This meant that mentoring capacity was stretched. Some mentors were asked to take on a third or fourth learner, while some new ones had to be recruited. By the end of 1999, over two-thirds of the Division's staff were involved in the programme with nine acting as mentors.

The pairing of mentors and learners was given some thought. In Phase One, where both came from the same team, the mentor was either the line manager or another senior person. Phase Two was more complicated. Learners were not allowed to choose their own mentors as this could have led to overload for some and a paucity of takers for other potential mentors. The senior management team, therefore, identified possibilities for each learner and offered a first choice mentor. If that match was rejected, there was a second choice available for discussion.

Where possible, although not exclusively, every attempt was made to match women with women and ethnic minority staff with each other. As Mark Wheatley explained:

> While this could be seen as either sensitive or insensitive, depending on your perspective, we thought it would probably add some value, especially if there were issues around race or gender.

Other criteria used for matching included the top team's perceptions of possible 'synergies' and/or compatibility of personalities. Mark then sounded out both mentors and learners on their potential partners and made adjustments where there were reservations. Over 90 per cent agreed to their first choice mentor or learner.

The programme is ongoing. Mentors and learners meet monthly for an hour. Occasionally there is some slippage mainly caused by pressure of work or fear – on the part of the learner – of being seen to be unprepared. Mentors are discouraged from agreeing to the cancellation of a meeting in case the reason given reflects an underlying development need such as time management.

The format of these development review meetings follows a pattern: the learner is asked to identify their agenda for the meeting; the mentor follows up any actions from the last meeting; anything (else) that the mentor suggests might be useful to discuss (with the learner's consent) is also included.

This framework also allows for: the discussion of any areas of anxiety or concern in the job that might be translated into opportunities; existing development issues; and for analysis of new possibilities.

The early meetings tended to centre around getting the learner to work through the self-managed learning guide in SMILE, reflecting on their personal profile, their competences, and what is required for the job, defining goals and coming up with an action plan for learning – a Personal Development Plan (PDP). The purpose was to get the learner familiar with and moving around that cycle:

> This general format encourages learners to reflect on the issues and to come up with actions. The mentor's role is to prompt them to decide what they are going to do about things. The objective is ultimately to produce a Personal Development Plan, work towards it, evaluate it and then move on to the next one. The mentor is there to listen, act as a mirror, prompt, encourage reflection, and to steer people towards ownership of their learning and plans of action. It is then up to the learner to decide what is best for or important to them.

The success of the programme is monitored in several ways. Mark checks up informally that meetings have taken place. A 'support mechanism' has also been established with separate meetings for mentors and learners, chaired by Mark, every couple of months, where they discuss SMILE, talk of their expectations, raise queries, exchange views. The meetings are carefully managed so as not to betray any confidences. This is an informal way of picking up what is actually happening and what is not happening. Mark is also available, on a one-to-one basis, to answer queries and to discuss issues such as the mentor–learner relationship, the line manager's support for the PDP and how to get back on track, where necessary.

Evaluation has been done using a 360-degree feedback questionnaire to check on the process and to gather views about mentors' skills and attributes. The results of this have been compared to a 'norm' group and the results discussed with mentors to aid their own development and growth.

While relationships between mentors and learners are confidential, as is the content of their meetings, it is evident that SMILE and the mentoring programme have been welcomed, are embraced and are working well. Some people have found their relationships quick to establish; others have taken longer to appreciate their value. Only a couple of relationships have 'broken down', where the mentor was too keen to give advice and/or less interested in listening.

Although the programme is essentially a mentoring one, coaching has occasionally crept in. Some mentors have coached their learners through the SMILE process showing how it might best be used. Occasionally, a mentor might make specific suggestions where the learner, after much reflection, has not found a way forward themselves. This would be very much in the context of 'This is what I might do. This might work for me, but it might not work for you...' As the idea is that you get learners to suggest things for themselves, problem solving for learners is discouraged, while any intervention by the mentor with the line manager on behalf of the learner is 'positively frowned upon'.

The role of the outside mentor at Sandwell

Mark described his relationship with the external mentor thus:

> ... virtually no coaching, effectively acting as a mirror, but cracking the pace and getting me through the SMILE process. A lot of issues that we discussed arose because of my particular concerns about the job or career. I had managed to do a lot of preparatory work beforehand as I had previously been involved in a management development programme that had involved mentoring, 360-degree feedback, analysis of learning styles, etc.
>
> My approach this time was to follow the SMILE process slavishly so that I could pass it on, mentor others and advise people if they came to me with difficulties.
>
> The mentor acted as a mirror, but was also pretty challenging, which was what I needed. He was good at pursuing actions that I had agreed to and was obviously very experienced at picking up the underlying

issues. He is good at listening and at intervening to focus me back on the SMILE process.

Success depends upon the learner and their motives for joining the scheme. I certainly treated SMILE seriously, regarding it as something for my whole development. We are all volunteers, no one has been press-ganged.

Benefits of self-managed learning

For the Division, the mentoring programme and self-managed learning have had many benefits.

It has encouraged people to reflect on the wide range of learning opportunities available to attain goals:

> ... just getting people to think more flexibly about the opportunities that are out there, about learning, about developing themselves and about the pros and cons of where they are at the moment has been very advantageous and has contributed much to morale.

It has also improved the capacity for individuals to deal with change:

> There is a potential organizational change on the cards which I feel some people in this Division would have found inherently threatening. However, I have not noticed the kind of reaction I would have expected. That could be the mentoring process or it could be down to the way that we have attempted to manage it. It could show a cultural shift. Mentoring contributes to people's comfort with change and gives a greater sense of self-determination.

SMILE has proven to be a workable system of self-managed learning:

> a sense that we have something sustainable, a robust framework that generates confidence... a virtuous circle involving the majority of the Division.

The mentoring programme has helped to plug communication deficits:

> The process can expose a few gaps, for example, where line managers are not making it clear to staff what is expected of them. It has helped to identify where some of the basics have been neglected.

The programme has increased learning opportunities:

> For some managers, it has added to their interpersonal skills and some
> have chosen to pursue a mentoring qualification, showing that they
> see the value in being skilled mentors.

The programme has increased cohesiveness of the Division:

> The programme has also made a contribution to a 'one-Division' feel.

Personally, for Mark Wheatley as a learner, the benefits have been that:

> Something is happening on a regular basis that forces me to
> concentrate on my personal development – the constant cycle, the
> discipline. It has also improved my listening skills by putting me into
> situations where I have had to listen as a mentor.

The disadvantages of the programme, such as there have been, have been minor:

> The fact that a few people have been disappointed probably because
> they saw SMILE as a panacea to solving all their problems or as a
> quick way of getting themselves a better job;
> The scheme was voluntary, therefore some who would have
> benefited a great deal did not put themselves forward;
> Confusion on the part of one or two participants who thought that
> SMILE was concerned with their personal aspirations, but not with
> developing them for the 'day job'.

Mark Wheatley considers the key factors that have contributed to the success
of the programme at Sandwell to be:

- that many staff are keen and aspirational;

- that mentors and learners were volunteers;

- that there is a framework which is smart, sustainable, robust and resilient;

- that the cycle is relatively fast within that framework, which ensures progress
  in bite-size chunks via the PDP;

- that mentors were fully committed;

- that there was an external mentor available to support and encourage the
  senior people;

- and that SMILE obviously encourages people to take responsibility for their learning.

So in the 'corporate' world, at least, 'coach–mentor' is the most appropriate model, but the quality of the relationships are the key.

Example 4   Mentoring in Spicer Hallfield

Diane Caswell joined Spicer Hallfield, a market-leading manufacturer and distributor of photographic accessories, in 1998 as their Managing Director. The company operates from three sites in central and northern England and employs some 160 staff.

Very early on, Diane set about introducing a new culture into the company that would, she hoped, involve individuals more in the development of the business and in their own future. She recognized the need to motivate, encourage and support individuals so that they could think for themselves, grow in confidence and take responsibility. The new culture – a coaching/mentoring one – also had to fit the business plan and be designed to help people to understand the business, otherwise it might be viewed as 'flavour of the month' and as an initiative in its own right.

The first step was to start at the top, by agreeing that the three directors (including herself) and three senior managers would be mentored by an external mentor. After three months, the programme was extended to allow another 20-30 key people (everyone in a supervisory, management or with a specialist role in the business) to have the same opportunity. They were mentored by insiders – the senior management team.

Preparation and training

Coach/mentors received some preparation for their role and did a lot on their own. They had their own three months with an external mentor and time to become fully familiar with SMILE by working through it.

Since then they have supported each other, shared reading matter, looked at how best to listen and ask questions, completed personality inventories, attended a workshop on understanding how their own personality traits might work/ clash with others, completed team inventories (like Belbin) and done some work on understanding themselves. 'They have taken responsibility for their own learning.'

In their regular discussions about the programme, they have shared some of the issues that have come up and which challenge them as mentors. They have explored when it is appropriate to be challenging with a learner; how best to work with a reluctant learner or one who does want change; how to make learners feel all right about the fact that they may wish to change jobs or move out of the programme.

Matching coach/mentors with learners

When the programme was cascaded and the management team started to work with others, it was necessary to match coaches/mentors (ie the management team) with their learners. Matching was done by the management team in discussion. They agreed, as a team, who would work with whom. Learners were told who their coach/mentor would be and had the choice of declining if they so wished. None did. Diane feels that this was very much the result of the careful thinking that the management team had put into deciding the matching. She explained the criteria used to match:

> It was based on 'best fit'... the personalities, different roles... We (the management team) matched everyone on a one-to-one basis... All coach/mentors were more senior than the learners... We were not necessarily looking for the same personalities. The main thing was that they should not clash so that there would not, for example, be an out-and-out extrovert matched with a very inward thinking reflector. The coach/mentors all went through Myers-Briggs first to establish what they were. In terms of roles, we tried to cover cross-functional roles because, in the business, we needed more understanding of each other.

The format

Coach/mentors meet with their learners for an hour about once a month on average. The detailed organization of the meetings is left up to the pairs. Some, who work far away from each other, prefer to meet for a longer session, but less often (eg two hours every two months), keeping in touch by telephone in the interim; others meet every three weeks for a shorter session. 'It's up to the needs of the individual. It was important not to force-fit a particular format on everyone.'

The meetings between coach/mentor and learner follow a similar procedure, based on the SMILE process. 'Everybody has a structure to work with, but where there is an element of flexibility, based on what the learner wants to talk about.' Action points are reviewed, the learner sets the agenda, anything that happened in between sessions and any reflection on that are discussed.

> The SMILE format is there as a tool. If you force people to follow it, it becomes a process and that is not what I wanted. I wanted coaching and mentoring to become a way of life.

Diane works with four learners herself and has been working with them for about nine months. Initially, her sessions with them followed a set structure – working through the modules in the SMILE programme. With time, learners' specific needs have become clearer and the focus of sessions has turned to address these.

Diane has found that some of her learners were initially apprehensive, 'nervous and in awe', about talking about themselves in front of her. They were unused to such an open style of management from an MD. This was also true when the management team first starting mentoring others. These feelings have now been calmed.

Monitoring and evaluation

The coaching/mentoring programme is not monitored as such. It is up to the management team themselves to take responsibility for ensuring that their meetings do happen. They are all highly committed and Diane has no doubt the programme runs as it should.

The programme is, however, evaluated in several ways:

- through a 360-degree feedback exercise, where all learners rate their coach/mentors on their skills, techniques and personal attributes;

- through learners' meetings to discuss how the programme is going;

- through having coaching and mentoring as part of the regular agenda at management team meetings;

- through discussion with the learners' line managers, so that they give the learners support, too.

Every attempt is made not to break confidentiality.

Coaching or mentoring or both?

The programme is essentially a mix of coaching and mentoring, using the SMILE package as a base tool.

Coaching takes place where a learner might ask for specific guidance on a task or where a person might be new to the business and needs to learn the in-house procedures. Mentoring takes place, for example, when a learner might want to talk about their future or where they might be going through difficult or challenging times at work or even at home.

Sessions vary, depending on need: some might be 80/20 coaching and mentoring; some the reverse or anything in between. The balance depends on what the learner *brings up* and what their needs are and the way in which the business is moving.

> We initially thought of the more senior person primarily as a coach, but the mentoring role has developed... There's a bit of both – a bit of mentoring in terms of helping learners to deal with different situations and there's a bit of coaching on the work front. It's difficult to say sometimes if they were coaches or mentors. People are doing different things depending on where their learners are with their jobs.

The role of the external mentor

The external mentor's role was varied. For Diane as MD, the external mentor was:

> ... able to benchmark our progress... to point out any gaps between where I wanted to be and where individuals in the business were... He was able to encourage me to take it one step at a time and to understand that any progress was good progress... He was a 'reality measure', making sure that I did not over-expect... His experience of other businesses was very important.

Members of the management team talked of the external mentor's importance in 'keeping them on the straight and narrow... keeping them focused.' He also had a role in helping his learners to confirm or explore whether they were in the right role within the business and whether their present jobs were playing to their best strengths.

Hugely important to all those mentored by the external mentor was that he was respected and trusted and so 'people were prepared to listen to him, he could be challenging in a non-confrontational way, making it possible for learners to get more out of themselves'.

The extent to which the external mentor coached or mentored varied with his learners. It was predominantly mentoring, but coaching was used when asked for.

Benefits of SMILE and the coaching/mentoring culture

Personally, Diane feels that the programme has given her:

> The opportunity to explore my leadership and management style, as this is my first time as a Managing Director and there is no one else to turn to... It has given an element of comfort... and confidence.

For the management team, the programme has helped them to learn:

> Who in their team can make a difference to the business... It has helped them to step back and ask 'Have I got the right people in my team to achieve the business goals?'

In terms of the business, SMILE and the coaching/mentoring culture:

> One of the big successes is that the programme has broken down barriers... Learners, if they have an opinion, feel that they can express it, without feeling there is going to be some reprisal. They now feel that if they have got ideas that we will listen to them... It has opened people's minds to the concept of accountability... You can't have empowerment without people understanding what they are accountable for. It has made them realize that they have to make things happen themselves and not rely on others. In terms of the company as a whole, it will take a while, but I believe there is already more trust, more sharing, better teamwork, a breaking down of barriers. People feel they can be involved, can express ideas and opinions for the benefit of the business.

The hope is that the coaching/mentoring culture will become the status quo:

> SMILE has been about moving the business forward, not an initiative in its own right... The initiative needs to be embedded and not be seen as a one-off... It is still very early days.

The factors which have contributed most to the success of the culture so far have been several:

- the commitment of the management team;

- the learners' willingness to 'have a go';

- a fundamental and passionate belief on Diane's part that this is a way of moving the business forward.

A recent visit from an Investors in People assessor confirmed that things were changing for the better. She reported finding a 'happy environment within the business', where people felt listened to, where they could trust their managers, where they felt valued and where they realized that they could make a difference to the business. People were thought to be thinking for themselves more and to be thinking beyond the task in hand. Diane felt this had come about through 'perseverance and hard work, and not by luck. It would have been easy at times to give up, but we are all very committed and have worked through difficult times.'

Each of these four examples illustrates the case for designing a model to suit the specific context and then interpreting flexibly and practically. The reader may now also have a clearer understanding of why we believe that the term 'coach–mentor' quite accurately describes what happens in practice, in both the qualification and corporate contexts.

The following self-assessment exercise may prove useful in helping you to judge your current competence as a 'corporate' or 'qualification' mentor.

Performance Criteria

Assessment Guidelines

There are three commonsense levels of assessment:

Good   which is above standard
OK   which is acceptable
Needs help   which is self-explanatory and is the information on
                  which to base a PDP

Stage 1: Confirm the Development Plan	
You identify and agree specific needs for guidance.	☐ Good ☐ OK ☐ Needs help
You ensure that information and guidance given avoid bias and take account of individual learning styles and the learning context.	☐ Good ☐ OK ☐ Needs help
You ensure that information and advice given cover choice of any relevant qualification process.	☐ Good ☐ OK ☐ Needs help
You encourage the use of self-assessment to develop self-awareness.	☐ Good ☐ OK ☐ Needs help
You confirm that any development goals are SMART	☐ Good ☐ OK ☐ Needs help

Stage 2: Encourage Self-Management of Learning

You help to identify the range of factors that need to be managed to achieve learning goals, including the comptences and resources required.
- ☐ Good
- ☐ OK
- ☐ Needs help

You help to identify the causes of any difficulties that arise and encourage learners to work out their own solutions.
- ☐ Good
- ☐ OK
- ☐ Needs help

You ensure that the relationship with the line manager is never compromised by any advice and guidance you offer.
- ☐ Good
- ☐ OK
- ☐ Needs help

You explain clearly the range of support available to manage the learners' own learning.
- ☐ Good
- ☐ OK
- ☐ Needs help

Stage 3: Provide Support During Development Plan

You agree a regular schedule of meetings and establish methods of gaining access to you as and when need for support arises.
- ☐ Good
- ☐ OK
- ☐ Needs help

You offer, but never impose, opinions and suggestions and, where appropriate, refer to other sources of guidance.
- ☐ Good
- ☐ OK
- ☐ Needs help

You ensure that guidance is given in a timely manner, at a level and pace appropriate and in such a way that it avoids bias.
- ☐ Good
- ☐ OK
- ☐ Needs help

You conduct and conclude discussions in a manner that promotes effective working relationships.
- ☐ Good
- ☐ OK
- ☐ Needs help

You encourage mistakes and setbacks to be seen as learning opportunities and build self-confidence and motivation to achieve goals.
- ☐ Good
- ☐ OK
- ☐ Needs help

Stage 4: Assist in the Evaluation of Success		
You encourage formal evaluations of PDPs with line managers.	☐	Good
	☐	OK
	☐	Needs help
You ensure thorough preparation for formal evaluations by conducting assessments of the achievement of standards with peers and colleagues.	☐	Good
	☐	OK
	☐	Needs help
You help to identify any factors inhibiting the learning process as well as identifying any unexpected benefits gained during the learning experiences.	☐	Good
	☐	OK
	☐	Needs help
You offer encouragement and ongoing support to apply the learning.	☐	Good
	☐	OK
	☐	Needs help
You motivate individuals to set new development goals and help to identify any support they will need.	☐	Good
	☐	OK
	☐	Needs help
If appropriate, you ensure that the mentoring relationship ends on a constructive and positive note.	☐	Good
	☐	OK
	☐	Needs help

Figure 4.2 *Assessment of competence*

Chapter 5

Community Mentors: The Catalysts for a New Profession

Let us now turn our attention to the third broad type of mentor: the 'community mentor'. If we start by examining a particular example, we can soon see just how different the context is from the world of work and qualifications illustrated by the four examples in the previous chapter.

The focus of many community mentoring programmes is to help those who, for whatever reasons, are currently excluded from, or have so far never been in, the world of work and qualifications. So, while the process has many similarities with the world of work and qualifications, the words that are used and the behaviours required are distinctly different.

Dee Keane is the Training and Resources Manager for the YWCA and was National Co-ordinator for a programme that we believe captures the essence of community mentoring. She explains:

> A_2O (Young Women's Access to Opportunities) is a youth and community work programme run by the YWCA in seven locations across England. A_2O targets disadvantaged or socially excluded young woman aged 16–19 and works with them to build up their employability. Each young woman compiles a portfolio to show the skills she has and those she is developing through group work, training and work experience.

Each participant is offered additional support and encouragement from a volunteer mentor. Recruited from the local community, the mentors are carefully screened and receive initial induction training, which is a mix of information and skills development. The information is designed to enable volunteers to make an informed choice about what mentoring with A_2O involves. Throughout their involvement, the mentors receive regular supervision and ongoing training.

The tasks of the A_2O mentor are defined as:

● supporting one young woman through the A_2O programme (initially up to one year);

● discussing the A_2O programme and issues arising from it with the mentee (learner), and looking together at any problems to seek solutions;

● being 'on her side', guiding her through a period of transition.

The Programme also stipulates that the A_2O mentors must be committed to:

● meeting regularly with the mentee (an average of one hour per week) throughout her time on A_2O;

● participating in induction training and regular supervision.

In particular it is stressed that A_2O mentors need to be enthusiastic with a positive outlook!

During the induction training, volunteers have an opportunity to ask questions, reflect on their own experiences of having someone to act as mentor (officially or unofficially) to them, explore issues and clarify their own motivation. The volunteers were also introduced to a range of typical mentoring roles that they might adopt. These are set out in Figure 5.1.

The full-time YWCA staff also provide regular supervision of the mentor and the mentee, and in that sense might be seen as the second, but senior and authoritative, mentor. Mentors are encouraged to support each other through a 'buddying' system and have opportunities to take part in further training throughout their time with A_2O.

GUIDANCE PROVIDER

A direct provider of: information, advice, 'First Aid'.

GOOD PARENT

An adult role model providing: support, care, interest, concern, explanations, help to develop confidence and self-esteem.

CASEWORKER

Providing or acting as: liaison with statutory and voluntary services, informal referral, advocate and representative for the mentee to relevant agencies, negotiator, key worker.

LEARNING FACILITATOR

Providing: setting of short steps, checking up on understanding and action, helping mentees to acquire and practise self-management skills: self-knowledge, information, taking action, coping with transitions.

Figure 5.1 *Mentoring Roles*

The relationships that are formed are clearly crucial to the success of the programme, as Dee explains:

> The mentees often reported that the fact that the mentor was unpaid made a difference to them. 'Because I knew she wasn't paid to spend time with me, it felt like she really wanted to do it. Also, either one of us could end it without me having to leave A_2O – I felt more powerful because of that.' Others commented on the novelty of the situation: many of them have had all sorts of professionals in their lives – social workers, probation officers, health visitors – but few ordinary adults who will listen and take them seriously. The mentor offered a different sort of relationship.

The mentoring role that is particularly interesting is the 'Learning Facilitator' and Dee felt the key things that the mentees learnt were:

● that there are other possibilities in life, both professional and personal:

> I'd never met a woman who did the sort of job Lisa did. To be honest, I don't know many adults who have any proper jobs.

> Shona let me rethink my relationship with Chris. I couldn't talk to my family – they all think he's great and that I should be grateful to have him.

● that, with support, emotions and behaviour can be managed:

> I really valued having someone to sound off to when things were getting on top of me. In the past, I've got thrown out of school or a job because I went ape there about things that were happening at home. Shahnaz let me say terrible things, then helped me work out what to do about it all. I would have been thrown off A_2O ages ago if it wasn't for her.

● that a domestic/personal upheaval can be managed and survived:

> Kathy told me a little bit about what happened to her when she was my age. I would never have guessed – she seems so sorted. Maybe there's hope for me yet!

- that they have many skills and abilities that go unrecognized:

> Fiona was really impressed how I manage to juggle everything. I thought she was joking at first – no one's ever told me I was doing well. I guess I'd been taking it for granted – you just have to get on with it, don't you?

The learning process mirrored Kolb's *Learning Cycle of Experience – Reflection, Analysis and Action Planning* (1975), but in everyday language:

> Here's what's going on, we talk it through and then unpick it to make sense of it all. Then we decide what can be done – by you, by me, by someone else. We'll maybe test some hypotheses, rehearse some lines, practise some skills, get some information, then catch up on events next time.

The Learning Mentor

The Government recently announced the creation of a new full-time post in the state education system: the Learning Mentor. This development is possibly the most significant endorsement of the power of mentoring as a new approach to learning. It also signals, in our opinion, the arrival of a new profession. Initially this will be seen as the 'community mentor', but the connections with the 'corporate' and 'qualification mentor', and indeed with the professional corporate coach, will inevitably lead to the profession of 'coach–mentors'.

The published aims of the Learning Mentor programme (initially 1,000 posts) are to:

- Ensure, through the recruitment of a network of professionally trained Learning Mentors, that every pupil of secondary school age in eligible schools in the Excellence in Cities areas will have access to a new resource focused on removing barriers to the pupil's individual learning, both in school and outside.

- Target help on those who need it most in deprived areas, especially those experiencing multiple disadvantage.

- Raise standards and reduce truancy and exclusion in the target areas, and to help local education authorities and schools to make accelerated progress in their achievement of truancy, exclusions and other relevant targets.

- Provide a complementary service to existing teachers and pastoral staff in school and others providing services to children and their families outside school, such as social and youth services, the Education Welfare Service, the Probation and Careers Service and business, community and voluntary workers.

These are ambitious and wide-ranging objectives and are backed by substantial government funding. They encourage our belief that they could well provide a catalyst to the merger with other mentoring and coaching activities in the public and private sectors, including existing organizations like, for instance, the National Mentoring Consortium, the European Mentoring Centre and the Institute of Personnel and Development. However, the published personal specification, which is to be used in recruiting the Learning Mentors, highlights the differences in the way this type of mentoring is expected to be delivered. The specification states that the key skills and competences for Learning Mentors would include:

- The ability to engage constructively with, and relate to, a wide range of young people and families/carers with different ethnic and social backgrounds.

- The ability to work effectively with, and command the confidence of, teaching staff and senior management within the school.

- Working with others, the ability to assess and review young people and family circumstances and plan appropriate responses, drawing on in-school and external advice and expertise where necessary.

- A proven track record of working with young people, and an ability to see a child's needs in the round.

- A desire to do something worthwhile for young people, to understand their needs and to gain insights into how they think.

- Knowledge of, and ability to work effectively, and network with, a wide range of supporting services in both the public and private sectors; and ability to draw on a wider range of support, information, opportunities and guidance.

- Ability to identify potential barriers to learning and jointly engage in strategies to overcome these barriers.

- Ability to see the mentoring role as a long-term activity designed to achieve the goals in the learning action plan and not a quick fix/trouble shooting role.

- Ability to engage in joint goal setting with the individual child as part of the learning action planning process.

- Have time and energy to put into the relationship.

- Be up-to-date with current 'know-how'.

- Possess competences in the skills of networking, counselling, facilitating and developing others.

- A willingness and ability to learn and see potential benefits.

This is an ambitious specification. It also provides, or requires, the creation of an infrastructure of contact and communication, not only among Learning Mentors, but with others working in the public and private sectors. When this initiative is seen alongside other government initiatives (the aim of 3,000 business-to-headteacher mentors, the 1,000 volunteer business-to-business mentors for instance), the claim for the recognition of a new profession is clearly strong. Alongside these developments, it is also worth noting that many of the managers, who are involved in the examples of corporate coaching and mentoring that we have mentioned, have already sought professional qualifications for their coaching and mentoring. This strengthens our view that the new professionals may well call themselves 'coach–mentors'.

The professional development of these new Learning Mentors is only referred to vaguely in the launch documentation as 'initial (mandatory) training will be provided'. Given the ambitious scope of this new role, that is perhaps wise. But the danger is that a 'training course' approach will dominate the official thinking, despite what we now know about the limitations of this method for learning these types of skills and competences.

Another real danger is that, what we term the 'social worker/therapist lobby', may dominate the discussions on the nature of the necessary skills development and professional standards required. As our different theoretical models and definitions show, there needs to be clear sets of definitions and standards that are based on the context in which the coaching and mentoring occurs. The sensitivity and care necessary in the community context does not necessarily need to be transferred to other more robust environments. The 'social worker/ therapist' lobby may feel aggrieved that their profession is not universally highly regarded by some corporate or government circles. Historical prejudices will, however, need to be put aside. Discussions on future directions will be more successful if they mirror the atmosphere of openness, mutual trust and respect that are fundamental to successful coaching and mentoring.

The challenge will be to develop both new development programmes and a new approach to setting national standards and qualifications that effectively meet the variety of needs of the emerging profession. One aspect of these developments will be gaining agreement on the language and theoretical models on which the new standards are to be based.

The Learning Mentor initiative and the A_2O programme are just two examples of the 'community mentor'. However, they contain many of the key elements of all community programmes. Dee's insights help us to understand the similarities and differences between 'corporate', 'qualification' and 'community' mentoring with greater clarity. Undoubtedly, the basic four-stage process model of Analyse–Plan–Implement–Evaluate applies here as in the 'corporate coach-mentor' and the 'qualification mentor' roles. For community mentoring, however, the *differences* in the language and behaviours required are perhaps best captured in a model on the following lines:

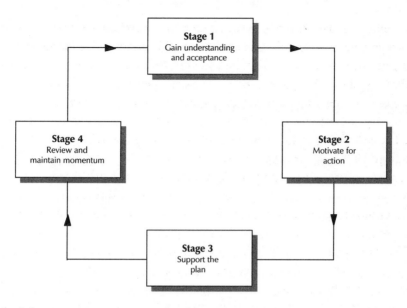

Figure 5.2

Stage 1   Gaining Understanding and Acceptance

Unlike the world of work where time needs to be tightly managed, the community mentor has to be prepared to spend as long as it takes to build a close rapport and gain a sense of trust and confidence in the learner, who is likely to be extremely cautious and uncertain. Projecting the right balance between empathy and firmness is not easy. The mentor also has to be able to provide access to a range of information and support agencies. So establishing the boundaries between the mentor's role and that of other professionals is key.

The issue of building trust needs to be handled in a way that demonstrates that the mentor has no hidden agenda and really believes that there is no right way of doing the things that the 'establishment' and those in authority are 'pushing'.

Helping the learners to develop a self-awareness and acceptance of their existing strengths and weaknesses is a similar requirement to other types of mentoring. The style and tone of voice requires greater sensitivity than is perhaps acceptable in the more robust environment of the workplace. The credibility of the mentor 'having been there, done that and lived to tell the tale' can be very powerful, for example for a young teenage mother struggling to manage normal but unruly children. That young mother may not respond well to someone who, although well meaning, comes across as yet another 'expert' giving her instructions.

Stage 2   Motivating for Action

Community learners often have a sense of personal inadequacies or feel they have already been labelled as 'failures'. Overcoming this negative self-perception and motivating them to construct an action plan to help to change their circumstances is no easy task, and the volunteer mentor can have a particularly valuable role here. Training and other support is required. The most effective method is probably for the mentor to role model the usefulness of keeping records, setting goals, reflecting on progress and making use of other support, supervision and training opportunities.

The key is probably the combination of firmness and encouragement with patience and empathy. Undoubtedly, a difficult cocktail of skills to be mastered. Setting goals, for instance, often needs to be taken in very small steps at a time and in a way that recognizes the huge difficulties some people have in mastering this discipline. Lack of patience and unrealistic expectations of the speed of progress is one of the main explanations of drop out and failure. In this respect, the contrast with corporate mentoring is probably most vivid.

Stage 3   Supporting the Plan

Having encouraged the learner to decide a plan of action that involves a gradual step-by-step route to a goal, the community mentor – unlike the other types of mentor – cannot simply sit back for a while and expect the learner to become a self-starter overnight.

A hand-holding role may sound patronizing, but being prepared to accompany the learner on their first visit to an after-school activity, the library or government agency may be just what is required. Providing support during a plan often means just 'being there to talk' on a regular basis. The most common obstacles to achieving the goals arise from life circumstances outside a formal programme, and the personalized mentoring relationship can be used to work through personal and domestic issues. The danger for the mentor who is too enthusiastic or too over-keen to be 'helpful' is that they may create a situation where the learner becomes too dependent on them. Striking the correct balance is not easy, and the availability of a mentor to the mentor (sometimes called a supervisor) can be invaluable in helping to manage this type of situation.

Stage 4   Reviewing and Maintaining Momentum

All programmes need to be monitored to review progress during the plan and to evaluate the outcomes at the end. Monitoring and reviewing is a constant process, but evaluation really takes place at the end of a programme or the completion of a plan.

In a corporate or qualification context, this may mean completing a skills development programme or being awarded a professional qualification.

In a community context, the achievements may seem more modest, but equally valuable. For instance, being able to open a bank account and to write your name on the cheques may be a huge success for someone who is severely dyslexic and who may feel they have been unfairly labelled as a failure by the education system. The need to celebrate these successes and at the same time to build motivation to set new goals is the same in all contexts.

A structure for a final evaluation session that has been found to work well is to ask the following sequence of questions:

- What did you actually do?

- What had you hoped to achieve?

- What did you actually achieve?

- Were there any unexpected learning points?

- How would you describe the personal benefits?

- What do you think you could do next to build on your achievements?

If the relationship has been successful, the chances of continuing progress, even without the formal involvement of the mentor, will usually be high.

The explosion of interest and activity in mentoring stems in part from the power and simplicity of the concept of a one-to-one meeting to help and to support the self-management of learning. As with 'corporate' and 'qualification' mentoring, theory and practice clearly collide in the complexities that arise from the relationships and the context in which the mentoring is delivered. It will take several years of real experience of community mentoring before an agreed language, models and standards are established, as we indicate in Figure 5.3 below, but the rewards will repay the effort.

Models of Coaching and Mentoring

Models are only useful in helping us to understand the connections between ideas and activities, and for comparing when designing appropriate models to suit our specific contexts. These are our suggestions that indicate the similarities and differences in language, behaviours, timescales and therefore of the standards required.

Stages	Professional and Business Coaching	Corporate and Qualification Mentoring	Community Mentoring
Stage 1	Analyse for awareness	Confirm the personal development plan (PDP)	Gain understanding and acceptance
Stage 2	Plan for responsibility	Encourage the self-management of learning	Movitate for action
Stage 3	Implement using style, techniques and skills	Provide support during the PDP process	Support the plan
Stage 4	Evaluate for success	Assist in the evaluation of success	Review and maintain momentum

Figure 5.3 *Models of Coaching and Mentoring*

Chapter 6

Feedback that Builds Confidence and Success

At its most basic, the success of coaching and mentoring depends largely on the quality of communication between the people involved. Workplace communication has long been recognized as an important topic, while two decades ago it was treated largely as a matter of language and techniques. People were trained in presentation skills, letter or report writing and telephone techniques. Today this is recognized as inadequate. The topic is now often termed 'interpersonal communication' and covers a wide area of understanding about how humans interact.

Effective communication still depends on the correct choice of words and methods. A logical structure, with the right level of content, the manner, tone and pace of delivery are still important. However, it is now recognized that more breakdowns in communication occur because of psychological relationships than because of the 'mechanics' of communication.

Put simply, people bring to any communication situation a whole range of important 'filters' that can distort the reception, understanding, acceptance and response to messages. The following diagram (Figure 6.1) aims to simplify some of these complex interactions by highlighting some of the key 'filter factors' that messages have to pass through on their two-way flow between senders and receivers.

SENDER ◀━━━━▶ **FILTERS** ◀━━━━▶ **RECEIVERS**

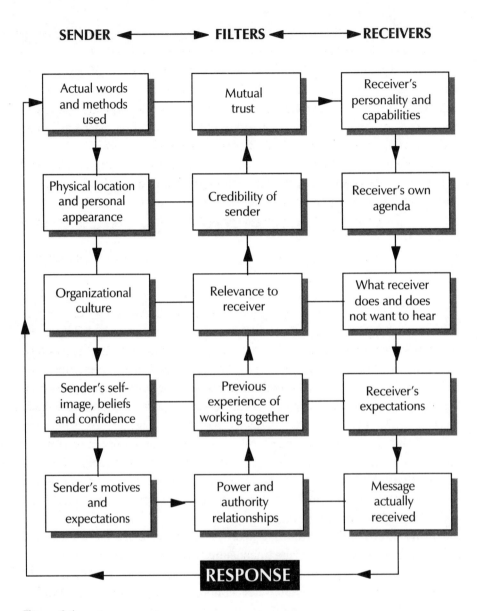

Figure 6.1

The diagram is one dimensional and perhaps suggests a systematic and linear flow through the process. In practice, interpersonal communication is not so smooth and many of the filters interact with each other in different ways, depending on the specific situation. For our purpose of becoming effective coaches and mentors, the main lesson is not to underestimate the sensitivity and care that is necessary to achieve mutual understanding, acceptance and motivation to respond positively to messages we send and receive.

One interesting definition of human communication is 'the passing and receiving of messages between two or more people in order that both sender and receiver may act appropriately on their interpretation of the messages they receive'. The beauty of this definition is that it stresses that communication is a two-way process that leads to appropriate action. However, it also emphasizes the equal importance of responding to sending and that feedback is fundamental to effective communication.

In the context of coaching and mentoring to develop learners and their performance, it is not an exaggeration to describe feedback as 'the fuel that drives improved performance'. Feedback can drive motivation to continue and develop in two directions. Get it wrong and motivation goes backwards fast. Get it right and motivation goes forward steadily towards achieving the goal.

Feedback is communication with a person that gives information about how their behaviour is perceived by others and the effect it has on them. Feedback helps us to learn by increasing awareness of both what we are doing and how we are doing it. Being able to seek and receive feedback about performance is therefore an important skill for the learner, too. If sought and accepted, it will greatly increase their self-awareness by helping to build a more accurate picture of how they are perceived, and it will help them to monitor the progress of their learning and development.

Coaches and mentors will continually find themselves having to give feedback. Inexperienced learners often want to ask 'How well am I doing?' or 'Have I improved my competence?' An experienced learner, attempting to improve their performance still further, might say 'If I do it this way, I think it will be better. What do you think?' A mentor may be asked 'I have the chance to apply for this new job, do you think I should do it?' Deciding on the appropriate feedback in these situations needs careful thought and should be based on the following principles. The first response should aim to encourage the learner to articulate their own answer to the question. The second response should aim to establish just how important or relevant the coach or mentor's feedback will be. Having encouraged self-assessment, the aim should then be to give feedback which is clear, concise and constructive.

Constructive feedback increases self-awareness, offers options as well as opinions and encourages self-development. It does not only mean giving positive feedback on what a learner has done well. Feedback about poor performance, given skilfully, can be equally useful and important as an aid to development. Feedback may well result in people:

- understanding more about how they come across to others;

- choosing to change;

- keeping their behaviour on target to achieve good results;

- becoming more effective.

Potential Barriers to Effective Feedback

There are several barriers to both giving and receiving effective feedback:

- Feedback can come as a surprise or shock when there are no clear objectives for the job or development, or when the learner and the coach or mentor do not share the same perception of these.

- The feedback may be delivered in a way that the recipient sees as concentrating on critical or unsubstantiated judgements, which offend against the recipient's sense of fairness.

- There may be a problem of credibility; it is important that the recipient believes the feedback-giver is competent to comment on those points.

- Previous history of receiving negative feedback may make the recipient feel obliged to 'defend his or her corner'.

- People are 'afraid' to give feedback because they are not confident about handling the response and are concerned that feedback will damage relationships.

Sensitivity and Stress

Many young people are shy and feel awkward and embarrassed in new situations where they have to perform alongside other experienced staff. More experienced people on a learning programme can also feel inhibited and unable to relax in the same way that they can in their usual work role. Helping people whose self-image may not be too high by guiding them towards early successes, encouraging positive behaviour and rewarding the efforts being made, will usually contribute towards the development of a positive 'I *can* do it' attitude.

Coaches and mentors need to be sensitive to the mental state of the people they are working with. Of course, they must also be sensitive to their own mental state because feedback is a two-way process. In stressful situations, people react differently and not always in the most appropriate manner. It would be a mistake to underestimate how stressful some may find the coaching and mentoring session itself!

Transactional Analysis (TA) is one approach to understanding the basics of the differing mental states that people have in relationships. A transaction can be defined as a signal or stimulus from one person to another, and the signal or response sent back in reply. One signal and its reply is followed by another, so feedback becomes a series of transactions.

Transactional Analysis suggests that there are three predominant states and that we all respond in any one of these, depending on our mood and the pressure of the situation. The sensitivity lies in recognizing, selecting or managing our own behaviour to respond in the most appropriate state to match both the situation and the mental state of other people involved. Briefly, the description of these ego states is:

- *Parent state* – which consists of our beliefs, values, attitudes, standards and morals. We calculate and judge in this state. We can also adopt either a critical or caring outlook to the other person.

- *Adult state* – which consists of our rational, unemotional and analytical outlook. We are happy in this state to consider reality, facts and figures. We readily engage in problem solving and discuss calmly the implications of our decisions.

- *Child state* – which consists of spontaneous, fun-loving and natural reactions to events. We are curious, creative and jokey in this state. On the other hand, we may act in an emotionally, irrationally petulant and sulky way just like spoilt children who can't get their own way.

The states could be summarized as parent (beliefs), adult (thinking) and child (feeling). People continuously swap and change between the three. Understanding the basics of TA and the ego states can help us to be aware of our mental state before or during a situation. This helps us respond in a way that is most likely to avoid clashes that occur when ego states become crossed rather than complementing or parallel.

The aim, in constructive feedback, is to get both people operating in their adult ego state, so that they can review facts, examine solutions and implications without crossed transactions creating too many obstacles of beliefs and prejudices or feelings and emotions.

How Would it Feel to You?

A useful way to begin to understand how to give appropriate feedback in content, style and tone is to consider how you feel when you ask for or receive feedback. Ask yourself, when receiving feedback from another person, do you:

- Listen actively to their description of your behaviour or performance?

- Carefully consider what is being said, trying to see the situation from their point of view?

- Weigh up the positives and negatives of changing or modifying your behaviour?

- Enter into a calm discussion about your views on their comments?

- Mutually agree upon subsequent action?

- Ask for any support or help you think will be necessary?

- Thank them for their feedback?

Be honest. In many situations there are probably as many 'No' answers as 'Yes' ones. By reversing the role, it is easy therefore to see some of the difficulties we face as recipients of feedback. We may:

- be afraid of what others think of us;

- wonder about the motives behind the feedback. Is it honest? Can they be trusted?

- fear a loss of face or independence even if we do recognize the need for help;

- lose confidence and feel inferior.

If coaches and mentors are sensitive to these issues and constantly remind themselves by 'looking in the mirror', they will avoid the pitfalls of insensitive and inappropriate feedback.

It may be all too easy for the coach or mentor to take the relationship aspect of their roles for granted, particularly if they have been working with their 'learner' for some time. In the work situation, issues of power and authority often underlie working relationships, the learner usually understands only too well that they are often in a dependent and somewhat subordinate role vis-à-vis their coach and mentor.

It is not always easy therefore to create a relaxed, informal and supporting relationship. This is particularly true if the culture of the organization is bureaucratic or aggressively hierarchical and results-oriented. Recognizing the reality of the organizational culture pressures is important. It will help both parties to develop realistic expectations. It is important also to appreciate the effects that differences in age, sex, educational background and different ethnic and cultures can have. This is not to say that these are necessarily or inevitably obstacles, but simply to point out that lack of awareness and sensitivity of the issues may make feedback sessions strained and unproductive.

Feedback that Builds Confidence

During a development process, one of the best ways to build confidence is regularly to monitor progress. 'How am I doing?' is a reasonable question that the learner will want to ask. For development to occur, the learner often needs to be reassured that they are beginning to perform closer to the standard or goal agreed earlier. Regular reviews act as a vehicle to reinforce effective performance, highlight areas for improvement and recognize developing strengths and potential weaknesses. Obstacles or barriers to performance can also be discussed and joint actions planned to overcome them or, if necessary, the development programme can be modified.

Whenever a development review takes place, it should start by agreeing exactly what it is that the learner wishes to discuss in relation to achieving their goals. If a qualification is the goal, how is the learner progressing against the syllabus or development plan? What do results from tutors' reports indicate? If the acquisition of new knowledge or skills is the goal, how has the learner performed in post-learning tests or in applying the information gained? A consistent, well-organized and systematic approach by the coach or mentor is one of the surest ways to build confidence in their learner.

Retaining control over situations or events is crucial for a development plan to be successful and some things are often outside the learner's control. For example a learner may find it difficult to resolve the reassignment of their work priorities to allow completion of the development plan. Their manager may be under considerable pressure to achieve short-term results and find it difficult to give priority to what they (the manager) may see as the learner's medium-term development needs.

To maintain progress and help to encourage a positive attitude, it is necessary to help the learner to develop strategies to marry their needs with the organization's pressures. Review sessions should also get the learner to highlight achievements and reflect on difficulties that have been overcome. Comparing progress to the original plan and recognizing the passing of milestones helps to show real step-by-step achievement by the learner. This also provides an excellent opportunity to reward and celebrate successes. This will, in turn, reinforce the growing confidence in the learner.

Aspects that the learner has had difficulty with should be discussed honestly. Was it the method or style of instruction or coaching that caused problems? Were the targets for achievement set too high? Was the learner trying enough or perhaps trying too hard? Were there sufficient chances to practise before starting the activity? By breaking down what may appear to the learner to be an insurmountable and complex problem into smaller chunks will allow each part to be simplified and dealt with separately and more successfully.

Visualizing Successful Performance

An extremely powerful way of increasing motivation and enhancing the will to succeed is to teach the learner how to visualize themselves performing an activity successfully and smoothly. Before attempting the task, encourage them to use their mind's eye and project themselves forward in time to see themselves doing the task in the way they would like to perform.

Sportsmen and women often use this technique and visualize themselves carrying out each action in slow motion. They concentrate on mentally rehearsing each step and then grooming it until it is perfect. Whenever the action is unclear or hazy, they rerun this mental video until a perfect sequence is logged in their memory bank. This allows them to relax when they actually perform and rely on their memory to steer them to a successful result.

In a business context, this technique can be adapted to help, for example, a nervous presenter. Getting the presenter to visualize themselves:

- talking fluently to the audience;

- hearing their words putting across a point persuasively;

- seeing their gestures adding emphasis;

- watching their amusing anecdote draw smiles and appreciation from the audience.

This will help build up confidence that they will be successful when they come to perform in 'real-time'.

Harnessing the Essential Mental Qualities

Building confidence then is about harnessing the mind of the learner. In Tim Gallwey's book, *The Inner Game of Tennis* (1974), he talks about the two 'Selfs' that are part of a performer's character. Self One is the 'teller' who instructs, evaluates and tries to control the performance. Self Two is the 'doer' who actually performs the task, often unconsciously and automatically.

In Tim's sporting analogies, you can often see and hear the two Selfs having a conversation! Self One is usually exhorting Self Two to try harder and to do specific things, as well as criticizing what is happening. This can get in the way of Self Two's natural flow and abilities by creating a 'busy mind' and distracting the performance.

For the learner, the danger may be that they try too hard and complicate and confuse themselves with too many of their own instructions. Poor results then encourage self-doubt to creep in, which can begin a downward spiral. The secret is for Self One to trust its other half and simply let it perform. Self One demands a role, however, so the learner must programme it with images of the task and of performing it successfully. Holding back on criticism and replacing this only with observation allows Self Two to make subtle adjustments and perform better.

John Whitmore, in his book *The Winning Mind* (1987), takes this process further. He has developed a list of what he describes as the 'essential mental qualities':

- *Responsibility*: taking personal responsibility for both successes and failures and not blaming other factors. Responsibility empowers the learner to take action, not wallow about in recriminations.

- *Awareness:* is most simply described as focusing on what is going on around you while performing. Being conscious of all factors in the environment and in the body allows the learner to self-correct their actions.

- *Concentration:* this involves remaining in a passive state while focused on the task, but remaining receptive to ideas and thoughts. By not trying too hard, the learner avoids the anxiety and pressure on themselves.

- *Relaxation:* is about containing Self One by keeping the chatter and instructions to a minimum. When the learner lets concerns about the future or regrets about the past into their mind, they also let in anxiousness.

- *Detachment:* involves the learner in standing apart mentally from the activity and observing their actions. Maintaining a free and flexible state keeps Self One at bay.

- *Commitment:* this aspect encapsulates the will to win in three steps. First, the goal must be achievable to the learner, second, obstacles to achievement must be eliminated and, finally, the will must be supported by 100 per cent of honest effort.

- *Trust:* by being fully prepared the learner can trust their own mind and body to reproduce the action or task. Self Two takes over the driving seat and lets Self One merely observe how well the performer has done – without judgement.

These concepts, although relatively easy to explain, are really quite sophisticated to apply and require careful study and practice. However, they are important ideas to master and employ.

A final tip for the learner, which John Whitmore advocates, is to find a personal stimulus that creates a positive and relaxed mind and to use it either as an outlet before performing or even during the activity. Examples might include listening to a favourite piece of music on a personal stereo or recalling a poem that inspires them. Physical activity, such as a visit to the gym or a short run, can have a relaxing effect, too. All of these techniques, Whitmore believes, help people to understand and capture the essential qualities of the mind and support a confident and positive approach by the learner.

Handling the Feedback Session

There are clearly a range of ideas and techniques that can be used to build confidence and the will to succeed, and the key is deciding when any of them might be appropriate. How the feedback is handled on a day-to-day basis is therefore crucial.

It is important for the coach or mentor to always try to balance the necessity for giving negative messages with positive ones wherever possible. Strengths should be balanced with weaknesses and the aim should be to be fair as well as totally honest. It also helps to keep feedback as immediate as possible. The question of timing is crucial, particularly if the session is likely to be disappointing – don't delay it, and don't give feedback in small amounts. You needn't mention every single fault, but you should concentrate mainly on the essentials. If you start with 'picky' small points, you may create an atmosphere that makes discussion of more important topics unnecessarily difficult.

If, as we have previously discussed, you are asked for your advice, you should give it, but remember, some of us like to give advice because it makes us feel important. Sometimes this only serves to satisfy our ego. Similarly, you should avoid trying to persuade or even argue. If the other person becomes defensive or obstructive, try to discover the reason for this reaction and build on that towards a positive action.

Be aware, too, that over-praising is often dangerous as it can confuse the situation. Being supportive does not mean constant praising. It means creating an atmosphere in which the learner can admit faults or fears, knowing they will be understood if not necessarily endorsed.

Always strive to be sensitive to the other person and avoid unwittingly denying the individual their feelings with hasty comments like 'You don't mean that' or 'You have no reason to feel that way'. It helps, too, if you can keep your comments as descriptive as possible and avoid making value judgements or giving the appearance of making a personal attack. Avoid saying 'What a stupid way to do it'; try rather 'On reflection can you think of a better way of doing it?'

Some tips are easier to give than to apply, but they will all produce a positive response. It is equally important to recognize that other behaviours have the potential to destroy the value of the feedback you give. For instance:

- being quick to disagree;
- being overly critical;
- being distant or aloof;
- interrupting repeatedly;
- ignoring comments, ideas, feelings;
- not asking any questions at all;
- appearing to be in a hurry to finish the session.

There are a number of things, too, that the learner can do to ensure that they get quality feedback:

- Identify who is best placed to provide them with feedback – managers, coach, mentor, suppliers, customers, colleagues. The concept of 360 degree feedback encourages an all-round look.

- Agree an appropriate time and place, when they will be able to have a constructive discussion.

- Be clear about the areas on which they need feedback.

- Try not to cover too many things in one discussion, but focus on the key issues only.

- Challenge the person giving feedback if they feel they are not being completely honest or specific enough for the information to be useful.

- Ask probing questions of the coach or mentor to identify what behaviour they should continue doing or stop doing.

Be aware that, although giving feedback is a difficult and unfamiliar process for some people, most will welcome the fact that you have sought their views and are willing to help.

Having sought feedback from their coach, mentor or another person, the learner must ensure that they receive it skilfully and assertively by:

- listening actively, concentrating and being receptive. This will make it easier for the giver to be honest;

- clarifying and testing their understanding of what is being said;

- not reacting defensively or trying to justify it;

- spending some time reflecting on the feedback received;

- thanking the person for the feedback.

Making Winners

Giving feedback that helps to build confidence and success is not simple. Done effectively, feedback is about the making of winners. It fuels the motivation to learn how to improve performance. This is your main aim as a coach and mentor. Think carefully before you start to give feedback. Remember it is fundamentally a two-way process. When in doubt, try to put yourself in the recipient's place or, to quote the proverb, 'Do unto others as you would be done by'.

The following checklist should help you to apply the essentials of giving effective feedback.

Checklist

1. Remember you get more out of people if you are sensitive to their situation and treat them as adults.

2. Imagine how you would feel if you were on the receiving end.

3. Make your feedback honest as well as fair.

4. Balance both negative and positive messages.

5. Don't avoid weaknesses, but always balance them by emphasizing strengths as well.

6. Choose the appropriate time and place as well as the appropriate tone and language.

7. Keep criticism simple and constructive by concentrating on behaviours, not personal attitudes or beliefs.

8. Encourage people to take responsibility for their own development.

9. Be well-organized yourself and hold regular progress reviews.

10. Recognize that you may be taken as a role model, so practise what you preach.

Chapter 7

Observant Listening

There is an old saying that God gave us two eyes, two ears but only one mouth so that we could look and listen four times as much as we speak.

Certainly, we have increasingly realized that talking is not the main part of the communication process. Not everyone appreciates this, however. How often have you attended communication courses, where the tutor spends most of the time explaining how you can structure your presentation or use visual aids but little, if any, on improving your listening skills?

More attention is also sometimes paid to developing your observing rather than listening skills. If you have ever participated in games or exercises, where several people are shown the same picture and asked to describe what they see, you will know that the result is often contradictory interpretations. All kinds of obstacles impair visual communication – and not just poor eyesight! People's expectations, assumptions, prejudices, values and wishes, all influence the messages they receive from observing and listening. Coaches and mentors rely heavily on these skills and need therefore to be able to apply them very effectively.

A coach using a 'hands-on' style needs, for instance, to listen to a learner's reply not only for accuracy, but also for the note of confidence or hesitation in the learner's voice. This will confirm whether they have really understood the coach's message. Confidence, and other emotions, will most probably be expressed as much in the tone of the response as in the actual words themselves.

A coach using a 'hands-off' style relies very heavily on questioning skills. As soon as the question is asked, the coach has to listen to and interpret the response and at the same time decide very quickly on the next appropriate question. Pausing to reflect on the answer given is often a sensible technique, but having to ask for the answer to be repeated because of lazy listening will damage the coach's credibility and effectiveness.

Mentors will sometimes hold sessions in their own office. Failure to take the elementary precaution of arranging for phone calls to be diverted can result in unnecessary interruptions to listening as well as signalling a degree of disinterest in the purpose of the session. A coach, focusing on developing a specific skill, often has to observe and judge actual performance in the workplace against a clear framework of competence standards and then immediately follow the observation with questions to check understanding. If awarding a qualification for the skill is involved and is to have credibility and validity, it is essential that any number of coaches observing the same demonstration of performance and listening to the same answers would make the same judgement as to the competence of the performer. So consistent application of these skills to a high standard is a requirement for effective coaching and mentoring.

It isn't Simple to Observe

The first rule of observation therefore must be 'it isn't as simple as you might think'. Observing is not necessarily a step-by-step easy to follow process, but is often continuous with lots of things happening at once. Take the example (discussed in more detail in Chapter Three) of the coach during a session with the horse rider preparing for a competition. Just imagine what that coach had to observe while the rider was practising even a simple movement:

- What aids did the rider use?

- How did the horse respond?

- What went well and why?

- What went wrong and why?

- How could it have been improved?

- Was the pace right?

- Was the rider's position right?

- Did the horse keep a correct outline?

- Did the horse resist and why?

- What was the general overall impression?

Take another example of a coach observing a salesperson in a sales interview:

- How did they greet the customer?

- What was the initial reaction?

- What type of questions were asked?

- How well did the salesperson listen?

- Which products were presented and in which order?

- To what extent was the customer involved?

- How were the sales aids used?

- Did the salesperson handle technical questions knowledgeably?

- How did the salesperson gain commitment or take an order?

- What was missing?

- How did the customer react throughout the interview?

- Which aspects of the interview went well?

- What could have been done better?

These and many other observations have to be noted as they occur. Learning to concentrate and interpret what you see is really hard work. Working with a checklist prepared in advance helps enormously. Note-taking is also essential; relying on memory means that important points are sometimes missed.

Taking notes is not easy for some people but, with practice, the skill can be acquired. Noting key words or phrases is one technique; mind maps is another. Having a sensible sized pad and a pen available is an obvious tip that is sometimes forgotten.

These two examples of a coaching situation also illustrate another difficulty associated with observing. Had the coach become actively involved with either of the instances described, it may have reduced the validity of the observations and subsequent feedback or assessment. Unobtrusive observation and restraining the impulse to intervene and take control, when things are not going exactly as you think they should, are therefore also important skills to develop if you really want to help people to learn from their own experiences.

Another danger to be aware of is failing to distinguish between an observation of behaviour and making an inference, or drawing a conclusion, about the cause of the behaviour. The following examples illustrate the potential pitfalls:

Observation	**Inference**	**Real cause**
John attended the meeting in shirt sleeves	He is unprofessional	He got soaked in a rainstorm
Wendy always leaves spot on time	She is uncommitted	She has a difficult childminder
Ken entered the figures in the wrong column	He is careless	The forms are poorly designed
Anne disagreed strongly	She is bad tempered	She is under severe stress at work and at home

Figure 7.1 *Observation vs Inference*

These simple examples point out how easy it would be for a coach or mentor to misread the situation. The guiding principles to follow are that:

- Observations must be objective – make an accurate record of non-judgemental, actual behaviour.

- Inferences are subjective – avoid drawing conclusions and stick to descriptions of what you see.

The Importance of Observing Body Language

Imagine a situation where you, as a coach or mentor, choose to hold a session with two people at the same time. This could be at the end of a project or before a programme starts. One of them sits with their arms folded, feet tapping and replies in a terse but perfectly accurate way. The other person is sitting forward comfortably, arms on the table, looking you straight in the eyes and answering calmly but in an equally accurate way.

If you are listening only to the verbal answers, you will receive one set of messages and quite possibly only gain a partial view of the whole picture. However, by observing consciously at the same time, you will also receive what are described as 'non-verbal' messages. These messages can be equally important and may give clues to either unspoken frustrations or important development needs.

To help resolve these dilemmas, it is important to appreciate the basics of non-verbal communication, or body language as it is termed. Facial expressions, gestures, posture, eye signals, body movements, all transmit a message. Body language, it is claimed, can be a window to our thoughts, indeed it often speaks louder than words – we may say one thing, while our bodies say another.

Some of the key non-verbal signs are:

- Empathy can be signalled by smiles, open and positive gestures, standing or sitting close, eye contact or nodding and tilting the head.

- A defensive or distrusting attitude can be signalled if someone sits with their crossed leg towards you, while a willingness to trust can be signalled if the crossed leg is away from you.

- Anger or aggression can be signalled by a rigid or tense body posture, staring eyes, clenched fists or clasped hands, tightly folded arms, foot tapping and finger pointing.

- Nervousness can be signalled by downcast eyes, hand over the mouth or frequently touching the face, shifting weight or fidgeting.

- Boredom can be signalled by picking imaginary fluff from sleeves, pulling at ear, stifled yawning or gazing around the room.

A useful book which will give you more information on observing body language is *Body Language* (1984) by Alan Pease. One word of caution: you will note that we have said only that these signals can *indicate* the different emotions. One gesture on its own almost certainly won't be enough to give the full picture. It is a combination of non-verbal signals that you need to learn to interpret. Not only must we recognize all these gestures in others, but we must equally be aware of our own body language as it may be interpreted by others in the same way!

It is also important to remember that, although people in the same culture or from the same country send and receive similar non-verbal signals, people from other cultures or countries may interpret them differently. For example, in the UK, people signal numbers with their fingers by using the index finger as number one. However, in Germany, if you put up your index finger for a beer in a bar, you're likely to be served two – they use the thumb to signify number one. Another example of cultural differences is that an OK signal formed by creating an 'O' with your finger and thumb means OK to the English or Americans, but to the French it means zero or no good at all! As an example of cultural differences, the eye contact rules used by Africans for showing interest and paying attention are opposite to those of Europeans, who often misinterpret this different behaviour as rudeness or sullenness. Styles of spoken communication can also differ markedly. Certain Asian groups tend to give very detailed responses, which are sometimes considered by non-Asians to be irritatingly long-winded.

One also has to be careful about other people's speaking delivery that may be affected by simple awkwardness rather than any attempt to mislead. If someone has an irritating or squeaky voice or speaks slowly or in what you find as a boring manner, it will be even more important to listen to the message rather then be distracted by the delivery. The message is what has to be judged, not the way it is said and this can sometimes be an incredibly difficult discipline to achieve. 'It ain't what you say but the way that you say it' can be dangerous advice to the listener!

Awareness of Body Space

There is another aspect of body language that should be considered within our context. This is the need to be sensitive to the area or space that a person claims as their own, as if it were an extension of their body. People tend to regard their office, desk, chair and the space surrounding any of their possessions as 'their territory'. To make yourself at home by immediately sitting down and placing your belongings on their desk may well be offensive and invasive to that person.

There are also what are termed 'personal zones'. These are usually determined by culture and therefore can differ. As a rule, what is termed the 'intimate zone' is that area very jealously guarded by us all. Move within 6–18 inches of somebody and they may well immediately feel uncomfortable and even threatened, unless of course you have an intimate personal relationship! Research has shown that people from the country need greater space than people from towns and cities. Another example is entering a crowded lift. You will notice that often, if it is very crowded, people tend to look up at the floor level indicator light, rather than at each other, mainly because they feel too close together. Research suggests that these behaviours relate to the very strong impulses that body space causes. If you want people to feel at ease in your presence, keep to the distance within which people feel most comfortable. An arm's length is a good guide.

It is also important to think carefully about the positioning of desks, tables and seating arrangements for a mentoring or coaching session. A competitive or defensive position may be created when a desk or table forms a barrier between two people sitting directly opposite each other. They are forced quite literally to take sides. This does nothing to enhance openness, trust and harmony. To avoid this, salespeople are often encouraged to move round to the customer's side of the desk when demonstrating or illustrating a particular point. This is done to create a feeling of togetherness as opposed to a 'you-and-us' relationship. It also allows the customer to avoid the salesperson's face so that, if necessary, they can look away with ease. This sales technique has to be handled with care to avoid the negative reaction of invading personal space, but it is a useful technique for coaches and mentors to be aware of.

Trust and Distrust

Eyes often give the most accurate and revealing signals of all. The expression 'we see eye to eye' indicates that agreement can be signalled by eye contact. Acceptable eye contact is usually in the area of 60–70 per cent during the course of a conversation. If the other person either hardly looks at you or alternatively stares intently at you all the time, there is a tendency to immediately regard them with distrust and suspicion.

It is claimed that body language can be the most important part of any message. Some estimate that it accounts for at least 55 per cent or even more. When the words spoken conflict with the body language, it is claimed that the receiver tends to believe the non-verbal message. For example, you are busy but a colleague asks you for a few minutes of your time. You easily agree: 'No problem, I've always got time for you'. Soon, however, you are looking at your watch and shifting in your seat. All the signals suggest you haven't got the time despite what you have said. If your colleague is alert and sensitive to these gestures, they will curtail the conversation and leave rather than risk upsetting your relationship. Similarly, how many times have you seen a child look at the floor and deny that they've 'done wrong'? You may be strongly inclined to believe the stance and gestures, not the verbal denial.

Myths and Prejudices

It is also important to guard against your own prejudices and to avoid stereotyping people when interpreting visual and verbal messages. Some people, for instance, believe that people with public school accents or who wear glasses are automatically cleverer than other people. Another common myth or fallacy is that older people find it harder than young people to learn new things, or that all women managers make emotional decisions while all male managers act only on logical and rational interpretation of factual information.

When you stop to think about these issues, it soon becomes clear that they are highly unlikely to be true, but there is a real danger of allowing stereotypes, or simply first impressions, to affect your judgement. In a situation where you are assessing performance against a standard, this can be particularly dangerous as you need to listen and observe throughout the session to make an objective judgement.

Of course people can try to mislead you. Someone who answers in a confident manner or appears to agree with everything you say may create a more positive impression on you than their level of performance deserves. There is a technical term called the 'halo effect' which describes this possibility. This warns of the danger of allowing one impression or element of the skill being demonstrated to create an overall impression that 'clouds' all the other evidence. Apparently we are all open to this type of misjudgement, particularly where one strong negative impression blinds us to an accurate and objective interpretation.

Active Listening

We have concentrated so far mainly on observation skills, but many of these issues also relate to listening. So let's discuss listening in more detail. It is useful to recognize that there are different levels of listening.

- 'Peripheral' listening is done at a subconscious level and can occur in formal or informal situations. For example, you may be in a busy restaurant talking with people at your table, but also picking up snippets of conversation from another table.

- 'Apparent' listening is what we all do most of the time. We look as if we are listening, but in fact we are not really concentrating.

- 'Active' or effective listening is often what we should be doing. This involves really concentrating on the message being transmitted by trying to understand not only what is being said but how and why it is being said.

It is the ability to listen 'actively' that separates the good communicators from the poor. Like any skills, effective listening requires self-discipline and practice and it is certainly hard work. It is estimated that most people talk at a rate of 125 words per minute, but that they can think at up to four times that speed. This means that as a listener you have a spare mental capacity that, if you do not discipline yourself, results in mind wandering and lack of concentration.

We have probably all experienced ourselves tuning in and out of conversations or discussions and then having to ask for something to be repeated because we have missed a key point of the message. A listener can, however, use their speed of thought to advantage. You can learn to use the time to mentally summarize what the speaker has said, to ensure you have understood the message fully and to consider whether you need to ask any further questions.

Success as a coach or mentor depends to a large extent on the ability to concentrate efficiently on what is being said, often for long periods. You may well make the other person feel unimportant or insignificant if they sense their ideas and feelings are not being paid close attention to. The relationship then undoubtedly will suffer. The temptation to only half listen is, of course, very real. Having asked a question, if you get an early indication that the answer is going to be correct, or is exactly what you were expecting, there is an inclination to switch off before the end of the response. By doing so, you risk missing some enlightening new information or ignoring additional information, which shows that your initial assumptions were incorrect. Similarly, you may be so preoccupied formulating your next question that you miss at least part of the response to your current question.

So what does active listening involve? What do we mean by active listening? The process is as follows: having received a response there is *interpretation* of what was heard, leading to *understanding.* Then comes *evaluation,* or weighing the information, comparing it with existing knowledge and deciding what to do with it. Based on your understanding and evaluation, you *react* by planning your reply and then you *respond.* Understanding this process will help you to adopt a disciplined approach to active listening.

What cannot be ignored in this process is, of course, the way in which a response is delivered. It is estimated that tone counts for as much as one-third of a message. An active listener must be alert to any emphasis on certain words, also to fluency, or lack of fluency, as well as by emotional language. In the same way, they must listen for the meaning behind the words. If a learner says 'The main reason is…', this could imply there are other considerations that may need exploring. Only by active listening will it be possible to identify and evaluate what is *not being* said.

Active listening requires planning and practice. We have to work at it and like all other skills, we need to be interested and motivated enough to want real results from our efforts. So, how do you go about putting all this into practice? Let us suggest a three-stage process for efficient listening.

Stage One

Carefully select the *location* (whenever possible):

- choose a quiet room or area free from the distraction of other people and noise;

- arrange seating to avoid any physical barriers such as a desk, but don't sit too close;

- set aside any other work you are doing;

- arrange for telephone calls to be diverted;

- remove or ignore any other distractions;

- shut the door, if possible.

Stage Two

Create the right *atmosphere*:

- make sure the speaker knows you want to listen to them, look interested and maintain eye contact without staring;

- give the speaker your full attention;

- address the person by the name they want to be called, usually their first name;

- be patient – allow the person time to say all they want to say (within reason);

- maintain a relaxed posture and encourage the speaker to feel relaxed;

- be encouraging by leaning forward, nodding, putting your head to one side, smiling whenever appropriate;

- empathize as necessary, if something difficult or painful or different from your own beliefs is being discussed;

- don't take any views personally and try not to be defensive.

Stage Three

Practise helpful listening *behaviour*:

- make listening noises: eg 'Mmmm', 'Yes', 'I see';

- pause before responding to indicate that you are digesting what has been said;

- keep an open mind – do not prejudge people, jump to conclusions, argue or interrupt; other people may have a different point of view;

- be aware of your own emotions; listen carefully even where you might disagree;

- suspend prejudice; don't allow the fact you disagreed make you turn a deaf ear to what is being said;

- concentrate on what matters by trying to get at the core of the response;

- be sensitive to mood, facial expressions and body movements to understand the full meaning of what is being said;

- plan to make a report to someone else following the meeting and imagine they are the sort of person who likes to know all the details of what you have heard;

- seek more information by summarizing, asking questions, repeating or paraphrasing;

- summarize to check your understanding.

Finally, make a habit of taking notes. As we have seen, listening only occupies something like one-quarter of our available mental capacity. The remaining three-quarters of the mind will wander if not otherwise used. More importantly, note-taking gives you a record of what you are hearing and helps to emphasize the importance you are placing on what is being said to you. Many of these helpful behaviours we have listed will be made easier by good and accurate note-taking, but it helps if you explain to the other person why you are taking notes.

Whether you are a coach or mentor, effective observing and listening is key to both roles. If you listen actively, your learner will feel listened to. The coach and mentor will want to encourage responses that guide the learner to work out the best way forward for them. The following checklist should prove a useful guide to improving the way you use your eyes and ears.

Checklist

1. Non-verbal signals are important and you should learn to recognize them in order to get the full picture.

2. Beware of cultural differences in communication habits.

3. Recognize that your own emotions affect the signals you send.

4. Don't let your own values, attitudes, and beliefs get in the way.

5. Concentrate and pay attention to details.

6. Take accurate notes to avoid misunderstanding.

7. Tone of voice is often as important as what is said.

8. If you want to understand you must be prepared to listen and show you are listening actively.

9. Establish the performance criteria before you begin to observe or listen to the performance.

10. Plan in advance to avoid distractions.

Chapter 8

Asking the Right Question

One of the oldest jokes we can remember is the story of the little boy standing outside the door of a house. A door-to-door salesman approaches him and asks 'Son, is your mother at home?' 'Yes,' replies the little boy. The salesman knocks on the door but receives no reply. After several minutes of knocking with no response he turns angrily to the boy and says, 'Hey, I thought you said your mother was at home.' 'She is', replied the boy, 'but I don't live here!'

The moral of that story is that if you don't ask the right question, you probably won't get the right answer. The combination of asking the right question because you know the subject matter well, and asking the right question in the most appropriate way lies at the heart of skilled coaching and mentoring.

Coaches and mentors should bear in mind that their primary role is to help and encourage their learners to develop. This cannot be achieved if they create undue pressure or confusion by inept questioning. A meaningful coaching or mentoring session depends on using questions that provoke a response that enhances learning. It is important to build a relationship that is open and honest, so that the learner can accept the sometimes painful process of being stretched by difficult questions. Asking embarrassing questions is likely to lead to defensive, negative responses and a deterioration of the relationship.

Developing good questioning skills is vital to successful coaching and mentoring. Many managers will, during the course of their work, have received training on asking questions on interviewing, appraising and counselling courses. There are also plenty of written materials and learning packages available. Let us nevertheless look at various questioning techniques, which every coach and mentor should know about and try to apply.

Understanding the Basic Types of Question

The importance of recognizing that there are two main types of question – open and closed – is amongst the basic theoretical concepts of questioning.

A closed question is one that may be answered by a simple 'yes' or 'no' and usually begins with 'do you', 'are you', 'have you', and so on. It may also be a question to which the respondent is offered a choice of alternative replies, such as 'Which of the following three alternatives would you choose…?'

On the other hand, open questions are aimed at provoking an extended 'free' response and might start with 'what', 'where', 'which', 'why', 'how' or 'when'.

Closed questions are appropriate:

- where a straightforward 'yes' or 'no' is enough;

- to gather or verify information;

- to confirm understanding of facts;

- to confirm agreement or commitment;

- to get a decision when there are only two alternatives.

The repeated use of closed questions needs to be avoided because a series of such questions can become very wearing on the respondent, and can quickly turn a discussion or session into an interrogation.

A more difficult skill to develop, but one that is essential to guiding and supporting a learner, is to use open questions that enable the questioner to:

- establish rapport and put the other person at ease;

- free up the other person to answer as they choose and in their own words;

- encourage uninhibited feedback;

- help to explore opinions and values in more detail;

- create involvement and commitment;

- check out understanding more comprehensively.

For example, if you wanted to ask a candidate their opinion on, say, the merits of the local football team, you wouldn't say 'Do you agree that the local team is a good one?' This invites a simple 'yes' or 'no' response. If you had phrased the question 'What do you think are the good points about the local team?', you would instead invite a response that required the candidate to express an opinion. If there were no good points, you then have the opportunity to follow up with 'Well, can you describe their weak points?' The benefits of using appropriate open questions are evident.

A Variety of Useful Question Types

Coaches and mentors need to exercise care in selecting the best type of question to use in different situations. They need to ask themselves some basic questions about the purpose of their questioning:

- Are they helping the learner to explore their situation in more detail?

- Are they encouraging them to move from an overall analysis of their performance to a more detailed one?

- Are they looking to help the learner to identify strengths and weaknesses that could be capitalized upon or improved for better performance?

- Are they working to increase personal awareness and responsibility?

There are several different types of questioning that are appropriate for different purposes.

Awareness-raising questions

If coaches and mentors want to encourage learners to develop their performance, they also have to help them to develop self-awareness, a sense of responsibility for future action and a commitment to persevere with the action. You will find that open questions like 'What happened?' and 'Why did that happen?' tend to produce descriptive and potentially somewhat defensive responses. Whereas questions like 'How did it feel when you were doing that?' or 'What do you imagine it would look like if you did it differently?' or 'What can you do to lift the performance still further?' will encourage responses that focus on positive ideas for future action. We would term these as 'awareness raising' questions.

Reflective questions

This type of question is a useful means of eliciting clarification and confirming that you are listening 'actively'. By 'replaying' the words used by the learner or rephrasing and reflecting them back you, as coach or mentor, can both test your own understanding and encourage the other person to talk more. You can say 'You said XYZ…, can you explain in more detail please exactly what you mean there?' or you can use questions like 'So is what you're saying…?' or 'Let me just check that I am understanding you correctly…' These types of questions give the opportunity for the respondent to give additional information or to think of new ways of making their views clearer. It also assures them that you have heard them and have understood correctly.

Justifying questions

These questions provide an opportunity for further explanation of reasons, attitudes or feelings. Examples are 'Can you elaborate on what makes you think that…?', or 'How would you explain that to someone else…? 'This type of question can provide very useful responses, but can also appear rather confrontational especially if delivered in a challenging tone or manner. Better, sometimes, to phrase them 'You say this, …am I right in understanding that what you mean is…?' or 'Could you help me to understand your explanation by putting it another way?'

Hypothetical questions

These are questions that pose a situation or a suggestion, 'What if…?', 'How about…?' These can be useful if you want to introduce a new idea or concept, challenge a response without causing offence or defensiveness, or check that you fully understand the implications of an earlier answer. Hypothetical questions can be very powerful and stretching in coaching and mentoring situations. However, they should only be asked when it is reasonable to expect the other person to have sufficient knowledge or understanding of the situation you are asking them to speculate about.

Probing questions

Effective questioning usually begins broadly and then becomes more focused on detail. Probing questions are those supplementary questions where the full information required has not been given as part of the initial response. The reason it has not been offered may be because the initial question was inappropriate, unclear or simply too general. Alternatively, the respondent may deliberately not be replying fully. Probing questions can also be used to discover motivations and feelings, where they have not been offered.

Probing questions are among the most difficult to ask and may, of course, involve asking a mix of open, closed, reflective, justifying and hypothetical questions. Their advantage is not only that they elicit more information where necessary, but they also help the learner to consider issues or factors that might be a little 'below surface'.

Two basic probing techniques are:

- *funnelling,* where you start with large, broad questions and gradually narrow the focus down to the specific information you are seeking;

- *drilling,* where you decide in advance the question areas you want to pursue and dig deeper and deeper until you strike the response you have been looking for.

Checking questions

Sometimes, it is necessary to check what you are hearing or to correct an understanding. This can be done through a number of different open or closed questions, such as 'Are you sure about that?' or 'This may generally be the case, but I wonder if it is true in your situation? or 'Why do you interpret it that way?'

Very importantly, however, it is crucial that the coach or mentor does not dictate the route of the discussion by 'forcing' its direction or be seen to be 'testing' through inappropriate questioning. Questions should be used to help the learner to work on their own goals and needs and to take responsibility for them. Questioning should not be used simply to satisfy the curiosity of the coach or mentor. Questioning is about helping the learner to explore possibilities and reach their own decisions; it should also be used to encourage self-development.

It is obvious, therefore, that a coach or mentor should always use simple, uncomplicated and understandable language and also to make sure they do not make unfair or unrealistic assumptions or jump to conclusions.

Types of Questions that Should be Avoided

There are several types of questions that are inappropriate for a coach or mentor to employ. They will not help to generate trust and they may provoke a negative, defensive or ambiguous response.

Don't ask…

- Long-winded questions – they will probably be misunderstood.

- Several questions rolled into one multiple question – people inevitably choose the easiest answers first and avoid the difficult one you really wanted to know the answer to.

- Leading or loaded questions – they usually only demonstrate what *you already* know or think rather than what the respondent really understands or believes.

- Trick questions unless you can explain the purpose – they can cause resentment and demotivation.

Examples of Questions for a Coach-Mentoring Session

It is very difficult to give examples of the type of questions that might be appropriate for specific coach-mentoring sessions, as each one will be different and will need the coach–mentor to apply their general theoretical understanding and range of skills to meet the requirements of that specific situation.

However, there are two techniques that may be helpful examples. The first is handling situations where learners are uncertain or unwilling to choose to face up to awkward or unpalatable options. In this case, the 'transfer' technique sometimes helps. The other situation is almost completely the reverse and the coach-mentor is faced with a highly experienced and motivated performer. In this case, questioning using the 'GROW' technique may be helpful.

Transfer Technique

It is not uncommon for a coach–mentor to be faced with a situation during a session when it becomes clear that the learner is consciously and/or deliberately choosing to avoid answering questions that will make them face an awkward or unpalatable course of action. The action may involve the learner upsetting a close friend or colleague, or disciplining a member of the team, or accepting that their personal ambitions are unrealistic or that their job is never going to be satisfying for them. In these types of situations the coach–mentor may believe that the learner's future positive development will only be possible if the uncomfortable truth is openly acknowledged.

The transfer technique involves transferring the responsibility for asking the awkward or unpalatable questions to the learner by using a phrase like: 'Can you help me by putting yourself in my position? If you were facing the situation where a learner was responding as you are, how would you handle the situation? What questions would you try to get the learner to answer or what suggestions or options would you encourage the learner to consider?'

We have found that, almost without exception, learners 'transfer' their behaviour, often in quite an assertive manner, and recommend a course of questioning or suggested options that force the issues to be confronted in a positive way.

In the process of 'transferring' their behaviour, they often very quickly recognize the reality of their previous reactions and often find it easier to resume the session in a new and more positive frame of mind. There is also a tendency to justify this behaviour change by using phrases like 'Of course, the reason that I didn't decide that in the first place is…!' At that point, it becomes easier to probe further into their real reluctance.

The transfer technique enables the coach–mentor to help the learner to free themselves from some of the inbuilt assumptions that are limiting their freedom to think differently. In this sense, the technique gets close to what Nancy Kliene in her book, *Time to Think* (1999), calls the 'incisive question'. She writes:

> Over the years I have collected Incisive Questions that made a difference to people's lives and organizations. Below are some samples. Note that the first part of the question asserts a positive assumption; the second part directs the thinker's attention back to their issue or goal:

- If you were to become the Chief Executive, what problems would you solve first and how would you go about it?
- If you knew you were vital to this organization's success, how would you approach your work?
- If things could be exactly right for you in this situation, how would they have to change?
- If you were not to hold back in your life, what would you be doing?
- If a doctor told you that your life depended on changing the way you lived, what would you do first for yourself?

These examples give just a glimpse of the powerful impact the skilful coach–mentor can have in liberating their learners' minds to think in completely new and potentially beneficial ways of the options that really exist for them.

The 'GROW' Technique

If a coach were systematically following the GROW structure (Goal, Reality, Options, Will) in a coaching session with a highly motivated and experienced learner, here is a selection of the types of questions that could be asked. These are taken from the work of both John Whitmore and Myles Downey, but adapted slightly.

Goal

To help establish the 'goal' that the learner wishes to focus on during the session, the following questions might be appropriate:

- What is the issue on which you would like to work today?

- What would you like to achieve by the end of this coaching session?

- How far and how detailed would you like to get in this session?

- Is your longer-term goal related to this issue?

- Is your goal SMART?

- Can we achieve what you want today in the time available?

- Are you sure you have defined your goal for this session?

Reality

To help the learner to understand more clearly the 'reality' of their own position and the context in which they are operating, the following questions might be appropriate:

- What is happening at the moment?

- How sure are you that this is an accurate representation of the situation?

- What and how great is your concern about it?

- Who, other than yourself, is affected by this issue?

- Who knows about your desire to do something about it?

- How much control do you personally have over the outcome?

- Who else has some control over it and how much?

- What action steps have you taken on it so far?

- What stopped you from doing more?

- What obstacles will need to be overcome on the way?

- What, if any, internal obstacles or personal resistance do you have to taking action?

- What resources do you already have – skill, time, enthusiasm, money, support, etc?

- What other resources will you need? Where will you get them from?

- If I could grant you one wish related to the issue what would it be?

- Do you need to redefine your immediate or your longer-term goal? (If the answer is 'yes', you will need to start the process again – this may happen at any stage!)

Options

To help the learner to fully explore a range of possible courses of action that are open to them, the following questions may be appropriate:

- What are the different ways in which you could approach this issue?

- What are the alternatives, large or small, open to you?

- What else could you do?

- What would you do if you had more time, a large budget or if you were the boss?

- What would you do if you could start again with a clean sheet, with a new team?

- Would you like to add a suggestion from me?

- What are the advantages and disadvantages of each of these in turn?

- Which would give the best result?

- Which of these solutions appeals to you most, or feels best to you?

- Which would give you the most satisfaction?

- Do you need to redefine your immediate or your longer-term goal?
  (If the answer is 'yes', you will need to start the process again – this may happen at any stage!)

Will

To help a learner to reach a decision on the course of action that best meets their situation and to establish the learner's genuine commitment to follow through with action, the following questions may be appropriate:

- Which option or options will you choose?

- What are your criteria and measurements for success?

- When precisely are you going to start and finish each action step?

- What could arise to hinder you in taking these steps or meeting the goal?

- What personal resistance do you have, if any, to taking these steps?

- What will you do to overcome these resistances?

- Who needs to know what your plans are?

- What support do you need and from whom?

- What will you do to obtain that support and when?

- What commitment on a 1–10 scale do you have to taking these agreed actions?

- What is it that prevents this from being a 10?

- What could you do or alter to raise your commitment closer to 10?

- Is there anything else you want to talk about now or are we finished?

- When would you like to meet again?

We should stress that these are examples only, not a checklist of the exact number, type and sequence of questions that must be followed!

Improving a Learner's Emotional Intelligence

David Clutterbuck and David Megginson have published lists of questions, in their book *Mentoring Executives and Directors* (1999), that they suggest mentors can ask to help build greater understanding and strengths in the five areas of Emotional Intelligence. A few of their examples are as follows:

Knowing one's emotions

The mentor helps an executive to separate the emotional and intellectual content of issues and develop an understanding of the interaction between the two by asking:

- What exactly happened?

- What did you feel before, during and after?

- Why do you feel that way?

- Is there a pattern here?

- Do you think you might see this differently as an independent observer?

Managing emotions

The mentor helps the executive to develop greater control of feelings by asking:

- Is the way you feel appropriate? Helpful?

- How do you think you should feel?

- How can you gain greater control over your feelings?

- How can you use emotions to achieve goals?

- When and how should you state to others how you feel?

Motivating yourself

The mentor helps the executive to envision the goals they wish to achieve and to plan how to get there by asking:

- What drives you to want to achieve this goal?

- What's stopping you?

- What will you feel like when you reach it (really good or flat)?

- What will you want to do next?

- To what extent is reluctance to pursue something a matter of a lack of confidence and how could you gain that confidence?

Recognizing emotions in others

The mentor seeks to make the executive aware of how their behaviour breeds behaviours in others and how to observe the emotional content in other people's speech and behaviour by asking:

- What do you think you may be doing or saying that might make your manager react to you in that way?

- To what extent and when should you be concerned about how others think and feel about you?

- Do you tend to get the same reaction from people in a similar situation?

- Do you think what they were saying reflected what they were really thinking (was there a difference between their words and body language)?

- How would you have felt if you were in their shoes?

Handling relationships with others

The mentor helps the executive to develop strategies to handle interpersonal exchanges in a way that is more likely to achieve intended results more consistently by asking:

- How did/do you want them to feel?

- How did you manage the conflict between what you think and what you say?

- What is your strategy for motivating others?

- What is your strategy for influencing others more generally?

- What is your strategy for being influenced by others?

Once again, this is not a checklist to be followed slavishly, but merely to give a flavour of how skilful questioning can help to develop awareness of our emotional intelligences in a way that promotes the possibility of behaviour changes.

Listening for Answers

Once a question has been asked, you need to allow the other person to answer. Another skill – listening – comes into play. You need to develop the ability both to show that you are listening (see previous chapter) and to stay silent and create pauses so that you can hear the answers.

Having asked a question, it is important that you remain quiet to give time for the other person to reflect and respond at their own pace. Many of us are frightened of silence; we have an urge to say something, particularly if an immediate response is not forthcoming from the learner. Try not to do this because it can be a real hindrance in any coaching or mentoring situation, where you are constantly aiming to encourage the other person to think for themselves on how to improve their abilities or improve their performance. Become comfortable with pauses or you may invite hurried or superficially convenient responses.

However, if your disciplined silence does not have the desired effect, you can either ask a direct 'closed' supplementary question, rephrase the question altogether or repeat the previous question in an appropriate tone. The important point is to get your timing right and, of course, avoid the temptation to butt in and answer the question yourself!

A Question of Style

It is important that you develop your own natural style of questioning. The most structured open question in the world will not produce the right response if it is delivered in an aggressive, condescending or over-challenging manner.

If, for example, you observe a silly mistake being made, there may be a temptation to blurt out 'Why on earth are you doing it that way?' The result may be that the mistake stops, but it is also very likely that the response you get will be defensive and aggrieved. You may have caused demotivation as well. An alternative intervention might have been 'Well, that doesn't seem to be working very well, does it? Can you think of a different way of doing it?' This is much more controlled – and is not always easy to think of in the heat of the moment. The response it is likely to get, however, is much more positive. The action will have stopped; measured criticism has been made and less defensiveness caused. The person involved has also been encouraged to think for themselves of an alternative and better way of completing the task. This process is obviously more time-consuming than a simple 'Look, let me show you' intervention, but the outcome is worth it. Again, the tone you use to ask this type of question is important. You have to avoid the condescending, patronizing approach as this will negate the effort you have made.

Getting the right response to your questioning is such an important skill that we have treated it in isolation. The following checklist will help you get the answer you want.

Checklist

1. Work hard to build rapport and put the other person at ease by adopting a friendly, supportive, helpful manner.

2. Be prepared to explain clearly why you need to ask questions.

3. Think about some questions in advance. However, do not be constrained by prepared questions. You need to be flexible enough to probe where necessary.

4. Try to ask clear, concise and specific questions.

5. Always acknowledge answers positively and in an encouraging tone.

6. Give answers real consideration before responding yourself. A pause will show that you have done so.

7. Use silence when appropriate (it may intimidate, so be careful, but it can provide additional, sensitive information as respondents may feel the need to keep talking).

8. Probe, where you need to, for extra information. Use phrases such as 'Is that all?' or 'Are you sure we have covered everything?'

9. Realize the importance of developing self-awareness by using questions such as 'How did you feel as you did it?', 'When and where did you think your performance began to improve?' or 'Why do you think you got that response?'

10. Always check your understanding by summarizing and using reflective questions.

Chapter 9

Managing the Relationship

The quality of the outcomes from both coaching and mentoring activities depends on the quality of the relationships between the people involved. Simply by reading this book, you are seeking to understand how you might 'manage' either your own coaching and mentoring relationships or help to organize others to do it successfully.

Research and experience suggest that many people choose their own mentors to help them to cope with the pressures of work and career development. Sometimes these mentors are partners, friends or professional colleagues in other organizations. In the world of sport or the performing arts, the performer often has a choice of their coach, too. It can be argued that it is more important that someone feels they have access to a voluntarily chosen coach or mentor rather than have one formally appointed. However, many organizations do not believe they have this option, for either practical or economic reasons, and see value in formalizing and managing the relationships.

In the corporate context, the question of matching a coach with a learner rarely arises as a serious issue. The line manager is most often the general coach by virtue of their role and other specialists are usually easily identified when specific skills need to be developed. When corporate mentoring schemes are established, as evidenced by the Sandwell and Spicer Hallfield examples discussed earlier, matching mentors with learners needs care. In community mentoring schemes, much greater effort and sensitivity is needed than for the more robust corporate environment.

The conventional advice given in the corporate context, where matching mentor with learner is done by a third party, is that it helps to organize it as a three-stage formalized process:

- Make sure basic skills and need profiles of mentors and learners are compared and matched.

- Introductions should be carried out by the manager of the scheme and followed up to ensure a working match is established.

- A mentoring agreement should be completed by the parties involved and a timetable of meeting dates and review agreed.

Matching skills to needs is a good theory, but it is important that care is taken in establishing the full needs of the parties involved. There is no magic formula and some improbable pairings have been known to work well. As Diane Caswell and Mark Wheatley explained, common sense and simple questions like 'Will these people get on and talk to one another?' may be the best way of matching mentors with learners.

We have emphasized the importance of clarifying mentoring roles, responsibilities and relationships. Everyone's expectations about the nature of the mentoring role should at least start from the same position. Some human resource professionals tend to exaggerate the difficulties involved in selecting and pairing. In our opinion, they tend to translate the issues of mentoring in non-work situations with disadvantaged, disabled or partly dysfunctional children and adults into the more robust environment of the workplace. We have never heard of someone's problems being made worse by a mentor simply asking 'Tell me about it'.

Acting as a simple listening sounding board is a skill most people possess. There may be potential danger, however, if the mentor chooses to respond by starting to give advice, as that is not the role of the workplace mentor. It is vital that when the mentor senses they have listened to a situation that is beyond their experience and capabilities to deal with, they should steer the learner as quickly as possible towards a more expert source of counselling help and advice.

Nevertheless, care needs to be taken before someone is volunteered or appointed as a mentor. The normal criteria or working assumptions in most mentoring schemes are that mentors should be:

- older than the learner;

- already qualified or more knowledgeable;

- more experienced in the job or longer serving in the organization;

- willing, able and suitable to do the job.

One of the strongest messages that comes from practical experience with mentoring schemes over the last decade is that while formal clarification of roles, responsibilities and relationships is essential, so too is flexibility. This is partly related to the value of encouraging informal and voluntary mentoring, but it also highlights the potential dangers of making uniform generalized assumptions, rather than taking care to define mentoring specifically in the context of your own organization.

Evidence from the United States supports the case for a flexible and custom-designed approach, rather than adopting a uniform theoretical matching model. Care needs to be taken in translating the US experience to the European context, because the US model for choosing mentors is one where the protégé (not learner) expects the mentor to play a significant role in promoting their career advancement. Nevertheless, extensive research by the highly respected academic Belle Rose Ragins had some interesting findings, presented to the EDM Conference 1999, including:

- Formal relationships cannot replace informal.

- Formal mentors are viewed as job coaches.

- Formal relationships may be less effective for women than men and therefore it is important to develop female mentors.

- Mentors in the same department as protégé produce less positive attitudes and less satisfying relationships.

- Programmes with guidelines for meetings were viewed as more effective.

- The type of mentor is less important than the quality of the relationship, and a high quality formal relationship was better than a low quality informal relationship.

- The method of matching and the voluntary nature of programmes were unrelated to career or work attitudes.

Interesting evidence from a UK source came from Richard Blackwell, Head of Training and Staff Development at the University of Nottingham. He wrote in 'In pursuit of the feel equal factor' in *People Management*, June 1996:

> Following departmental consultation, the University of Nottingham introduced a formal mentoring scheme for probationary lecturers and graduate teaching assistants on a trial basis in 1994.
>
> The model of mentorship and the balance between formality and informality are central to that process. Most prescriptions on mentoring implicitly advocate a hierarchical model of learning akin to apprenticeship. For instance, there is a common tendency to refer to mentees only as 'learners'. Some mentees at the University rejected this notion.
>
> Criticism of the model came from three sources. First, during the formal training carried out for mentors and mentees in 1995, several mentees argued against the prevailing assumption of initial dependence, advocating mutuality instead. Second, it became clear on the grapevine that some mentees objected to the term 'protégé as inaccurate and patronizing. Third, in a survey of the training needs of all academic staff, the mentoring workshops were seen as having had the least impact of any staff development event. There are, of course, a range of potential explanations for this but, taken with the other feedback, it seems likely that criticism of the model promoted in the training was a factor. But is 'peer mentoring' an alternative? The defining characteristic of peer relationships appears to be 'felt equality', which, in higher education at least, seems to relate to:
> * Age. The greater the disparity, the less likely individuals are to feel like peers.
> * Length of service. Again, the greater the disparity, the less likely is a peer relationship.
> * Status differences. Professors are less likely to develop peer relationships with new staff than with established lecturers.
> * Assumptions about sources of knowledge and approaches to learning. The more interactive and collaborative the approach of the mentor and, to a lesser extent, the mentee, the more likely the pair are to view themselves as peers.
>
> It seems likely that professionals in other walks of life, such as accountancy or law, who are not complete novices and are reasonably well-trained, may also develop peer mentors.

In business-to-business mentoring programmes that are part-funded by tax payers' money, there are usually three steps in setting up a mentoring programme:

- The person requesting mentoring is asked to complete a registration form, as the focus for entry into the scheme and subsequent follow up action.

- Their company is first assessed for suitability for inclusion in the scheme and a co-ordinator visits the person to explain the operation of the scheme and to build a picture of their key requirements.

- A simple business diagnostic template is used to establish the broad nature of the support needed.

The approach to matching in community schemes usually has to be formalized. In schemes like the government's Fair Deal at Work, which aims to help the unemployed back into the workforce, mentoring is mandatory and therefore formalized. Under the Prince's Youth Business Trust scheme, which helps fund new business initiatives, the 'mentorees' identify themselves by applying for grant aid. Mentoring is a mandatory part of the subsequent process.

The selection of mentors is also given a great deal of careful attention. Profiles of the ideal mentor for a specific context are often drawn up. One of the most useful generic profiles for a 'qualification' and 'corporate' mentor was produced in 1989 by the then Council for National Academic Awards and the government's Training Agency:

Good mentors are:

- good motivators, perceptive, able to support the objectives of the programme and fulfil their responsibilities to the candidate;

- high performers, secure in their own position within the organization and unlikely to feel threatened by, or resentful of, the candidate's opportunities;

- able to show that a responsibility for mentoring is part of their own job description;

- able to establish a good and professional relationship, be sympathetic, accessible and knowledgeable about the candidate's area of interest;

- sufficiently senior to be in touch with the corporate structure, sharing the company's values and able to give the candidate access to resources and information;

- good teachers, able to advise and instruct without interfering, allowing candidates to explore and pursue ideas even though they may not be optimum pathways;

- good negotiators, willing and able to plan alongside their own management teams and academics.

If you take this model and compare it with the example of Dee Keane's Young Women's Access to Opportunities programme, you will get another insight into the differences in the various roles.

Volunteering and choosing is not a one-way street of course. It is vital, too, that mentors have a choice about volunteering for the role. An unwilling or half-hearted mentor can do more damage than good. The following self-assessment exercise has proved helpful as a guide to suitability to be a mentor.

Mentoring Volunteer's Health Check

	DEFINITELY	PARTIALLY	NOT AT ALL
Tick the box as appropriate:			
1. Do you understand how mentoring differs from other roles you are asked to play in your organization?	☐	☐	☐
2. Do you really want to take on the role and are you willing to make the necessary time available?	☐	☐	☐
3. Are you comfortable in being asked to assess your own strengths and weaknesses, and relate them to the learner's development needs so that you can guide them to other sources of help where it is appropriate?	☐	☐	☐
4. Are you sure that you can invest time early on in the relationship to establish rapport and a regular schedule for discussions?	☐	☐	☐
5. Do you know how to enable the learner to produce a realistic development plan, and ensure that it is 'signed off' by all the relevant people?	☐	☐	☐
6. Will you be able to keep the relationship on a professional level, particularly where there are differences in gender (sensitivity to potential misinterpretation in language and behaviour will be important in these situations)?	☐	☐	☐
7. Do you understand the distinction between counselling and advising and, whenever possible, will you encourage the learner to work out their own solutions with you acting only as a sounding board?	☐	☐	☐
8. Are you aware that you will be a role model, and that how you are seen to manage in day-to-day situations will affect the relationship you have with the learner?	☐	☐	☐
9. Are you sure that the feedback you give will be clear, honest and constructive, and designed to build confidence and ongoing commitment in the learner?	☐	☐	☐
10. Will you be able to recognize when the time has come to end the relationship, and aim to end on a positive and supportive note by sharing the value you have both gained from the experience?	☐	☐	☐

Figure 9.1 *Mentoring Volunteer's Health Check*

If you have given 10 'Definitely' answers, you are an ideal candidate to become a mentor and should volunteer at once. If you have even two 'Not at all' answers, you should seriously reconsider your willingness to become a mentor. Most people will probably be somewhere between these two extremes. After careful discussion, and with a genuine willingness on your part to develop in any areas of perceived weakness, you should be able to take on a mentoring role with some confidence.

The Seven 'Laws' of Self-Managed Personal Development

Helping people to learn how to manage their own learning is the principle aim of coaching and mentoring. As we move into an era where 'taking responsibility for your own personal learning and development' becomes the accepted philosophy behind the psychological contract of employment, there are a number of 'basic laws' that coach–mentors need to help people to understand, accept and to take into account when managing their expectations.

We use the term 'laws' in a slightly light-hearted style and accept that each coach–mentor may choose to express them in their own words to suit the context they are working in. The main aim of these 'laws' is to help to ensure that the expectations of the outcomes of self-managed learning are based firmly on 'feet-on-the-floor' practicality. They are based mainly on experience of the world of work. As our understanding of community mentoring gathers pace, there will no doubt be variations to be made.

1. The Universal Law of Solutions states that:

> There is NO universal solution for 'people problems' except death. So everyone needs to become completely open-minded and accept a degree of 'anarchy' as people seek to find their own development solutions.

'Self-management' equates to 'self-government' and implies independence from traditional constraints. This will prove particularly difficult to accept for those who believe that good management and organizational efficiency requires rigid centrally controlled and uniform 'people policies'. It will be discomforting, too, for those who believe that everyone has the right from their employer to 'know exactly and consistently where they stand' and always to receive 'uniform and equal' treatment.

Higher levels of stress in the workplace are therefore inevitable as these conflicts and contradictions work themselves out in practice.

2. The Law of the Acceptance of Change states that:

People at work are creatures of habit and inclination. Faced with proposals to change working practices, you will find, *if you are fortunate*, that at the end of the first year of the programme
- 30% have become 'willing-adopters';
- 30% are at best 'reluctant-adopters';
- 30% are still 'determined-avoiders';
- 10% are 'no-hopers'.

Expectations on the speed of the acceptance of change should therefore be adjusted accordingly. During the first year of change, too, you may also expect that:

● The 'willing adopters' become apprehensive but remain optimistic.

● The 'reluctant adopters' become insecure and tend to be pessimistic.

● The 'determined avoiders' go into denial and behave like ostriches.

● The 'no-hopers' find the stress levels unacceptable and often leave or retire.

This does not make anyone right or wrong. This is just how people are. Morale and performance levels can also be expected to dip below existing levels before gradually moving to new and higher levels. So persistence and patience is the key. Quick fixes fizzle out.

3. The Law of Motivation states that:

People only take self-development seriously when they recognize either an immediate tangible benefit or a credible negative consequence of not doing so.

Choices of resources and of what, how, when and where personal development should happen, although important, are in practice secondary considerations.

4. The Law of Visible Reward states that:

People understand perfectly well what behaviour is rewarded in their organization. They will, therefore, copy what managers ARE and what they DO rather than follow what managers SAY should be done in terms of accepting responsibility for personal development as part of their expected behaviour during working hours.

5. The Law of Business Benefits states that:

Managers, who cannot agree and support Personal Development Plans that balance the ambitions of the individual with real business benefits, should probably be sacked.

This may sound over the top, but very serious damage can be done to morale, management credibility and to bottom-line performance by managers who refuse to acknowledge or, even worse, pay half-hearted lip service to the key role that 'planned personal development' plays in motivating and retaining good people in their organization.

6. The Law of Cost–Benefit Returns states that:

Personal Development Programmes rarely produce quantitative results that will satisfy the narrow 'accountant mentality'.

Therefore you should stop trying to measure the unmeasureable and put your trust instead in accountability through rigorous self-assessment and discussion of what people actually do in practice compared to the expected and acceptable performance standards.

7. The Law of Client (and Personal) Satisfaction states that:

You should only agree 'contracts' with your colleagues, your bosses or external clients who understand, accept and are genuinely trying to live in accordance with Laws 1–6. If you have the misfortune to work for a boss who absolutely refuses to accept this law, then you should probably try to change your job!

These 'laws' may be expressed a little light-heartedly but they contain important truths. The last 'law' in particular addresses the issue of achieving satisfaction and value from the helping and supporting relationship. If these 'laws' are discussed openly at the start of the relationship the underlying assumptions and mutual expectations will have been 'surfaced'.

The value of 'surfacing' feelings and emotions, while uncomfortable to those unfamiliar with process, should be an important part of any mentoring programme. It is a technique for developing a deeper understanding of both the learner and the coach–mentor.

In the early stages of any relationship, both parties are inclined to make judgements and form assumptions on the basis of the behaviours they can observe and their interpretations of the words they hear. Behind these behaviours lie a mass of motives, emotions, values, beliefs, attitudes and even genetic differences, to mention only a few of the factors that impact on the words and actions used. These factors usually lie unrecognized beneath the surface. However, by managing a process that allows them to be openly discussed and debated they can be usefully 'surfaced'.

Dr Peter Honey is one powerful advocate of the value of this technique. To demonstrate his own commitment to the process, he publishes his own values about learning to his own staff and to anyone interested in knowing 'where he is coming from' (he even prints them on postcards of his own paintings !). His published values are:

- Learning, as a topic, supersedes all others.

- Everyone has a basic right to learn and develop and be supported and encouraged to do so.

- There is no more important task than helping people to take responsibility for their own learning and development.

- Since it is just as easy to learn wrong things as it is to learn right things, what constitutes good learning needs to be debated and agreed.

- You are what you learn; all you know, all your skills, all your beliefs have to be learnt.

- Learning is a skill that, like any other skill, you can develop and improve; learning to learn is the ultimate skill.

- Learning is only effective when you convert it into improved performance.

- You need to supplement your tacit 'intuitive' learning with explicit 'conscious' learning that is clear and communicable.

- At work, learning and achieving are twin priorities.

- Reviewing is the gateway to appropriate learning and action.

- It is your duty to share your learning and share best practice.

Peter does not suggest that these are the holy grail of values about learning, merely that he has 'surfaced' his own. We recently attended a session where Peter demonstrated another 'surfacing' technique with a group of 30 coach–mentors drawn from widely different environments in the corporate and community sectors. He divided the group into four smaller groups and gave them a pack of 50 cards, each containing a statement of an important belief relating to effective coaching. The groups were asked to sort the cards choosing only the 12 most important statements. These choices were then compared and a priority list established for all 30 coach–mentors. The discussions during this process 'surfaced' a high degree of shared beliefs and underlying values. In this instance the most important beliefs on the role of a coach were to:

100 per cent agreement:

- encourage the learner to take responsibility for their own learning and development;

75 per cent agreement:

- make time for coaching;

- actively listen to the learner;

- establish rapport with the learner;

- show a genuine interest in what the learner wants to achieve;

- help the learner work things out for themselves;

- avoid jumping to conclusion/being judgemental;

- explore options – the advantages and disadvantages of different courses of actions;

- encourage the learner to reflect on specific experiences in order to draw learning from them.

50 per cent agreement:

- establish what help the learner wants/needs;

- be reliable: keeps previously arranged appointments with the learner;

- show empathy with the learner (be able to see things from the learner's point of view);

- ask questions to get the learner to explore issues more deeply;

- explore learner's ideas without imposing own views;

- give support and encouragement;

- help the learner understand the effects of their behaviour on others;

- encourage the learner to set learning objectives;

- help the learner identify/prioritize their development needs.

25 per cent agreement:

- accept feedback/criticism from the learner without being defensive/resentful;

- draw out understanding (as opposed to spoon-feeding);

- stimulate/fire the learner's imagination;

- provide constructive feedback;

- steer the learner towards realistic courses of action;

- encourage the learner to have ongoing personal development plans.

Again, this is only an example for one group. However, similar techniques used on a one-to-one basis can provide the basis for a clear understanding of mutual expectations about the relationship.

A different approach to achieve a similar objective has been followed by the Working Party to establish National Standards for Mentoring, led by Ann Reynard of the University of North London. At the time of writing, the Working Party has produced a draft 'Ethical Code of Practice for Mentoring'. This draft is very likely to be amended as a result of widespread consultation, but it is a useful guide to thinking that stems largely from the community and academic viewpoint. The Code suggests:

- The mentor's role is to respond to the mentee's needs and agenda; it is not to impose their own agenda.

- Mentors must work within the current agreement with the mentee about confidentiality that is appropriate within the context.

- Mentors must be aware of any current law and work within the law.

- Mentor and mentee must be aware that computer-based records are subject to statutory regulations under the Data Protection Act 1984.

- The mentee should be aware of their rights and any complaints procedures.

- Mentors and mentees should respect each other's time and other responsibilities, ensuring that they do not impose beyond what is reasonable.

- The mentee must accept increasing responsibility for managing the relationship; the mentor should empower them to do so and must generally promote the learner's autonomy.

- Either party may dissolve the relationship. However, both the mentor and the mentee have the responsibility to discuss the matter together, as part of mutual learning.

- Mentors need to be aware of the limits of their own competence in the practice of mentoring.

- The mentor will not intrude into areas the mentee wishes to keep private until invited to do so. However, they should help the mentee to recognize how other issues may relate to these areas.

- Mentors and mentee should aim to be open and truthful with each other and themselves about the relationship itself.

- Mentors and mentee share the responsibility for the smooth winding down of the relationship when it has achieved its purpose – they must avoid creating dependency.

- The mentoring relationship must not be exploitative in any way, neither must it be open to misinterpretation.

This 'Ethical Code of Practice' will eventually become the national standard adopted by the government. Its main use will be to act as a guide to anyone running a mentoring scheme on how to help to establish a 'contract' at the start of a relationship. To some, this may seem over complicated and to others perhaps not comprehensive enough. Once again, the context is all. So too, we believe, is the value of simplicity.

The Seven Golden Rules of Simplicity

The seven 'Laws of Self-Managed Personal Development' are clearly derived from our years of experience in the world of work. Based on that experience, too, we have developed what we term the 'Golden Rules of Simplicity'. Modestly we suggest, however, that these rules might also be applied to good effect in some of the community contexts where coaching and mentoring relationships need to be managed.

Simplicity Rule 1   'Success comes most surely from doing simple things consistently'

We have met very few people who cannot become good, competent and useful coaches and mentors. The key to success is not to over-complicate the roles or to erect unrealistic and unnecessary barriers and expectations. Following our other six 'Rules of Simplicity' reflects an approach that provides the basis for successful coaching and mentoring relationships.

Simplicity Rule 2 'Make sure you meet'

By far the most common reason why coaching and mentoring schemes fail is that the busy coach–mentor, volunteer or manager, doesn't find the time to meet with their learners. Of course, time pressures are intense on everyone and arguably have intensified in recent years. However, we all have the same time available to us. So the issue is really what we choose to do with it and what tools can we use to help us to find the necessary 'extra' time?

The tool most commonly used to help to manage our time is, of course, the diary. We strongly advocate the use of some form of learning and/or planning diary in which both coach–mentor and learner commit to each other to meet on a specific day and time each month. The simple act of mutually writing the commitment down increases the likelihood of it happening – but be honest. If you don't intend to keep the commitment, don't write it down.

No manager can advocate the necessity for others to take personal responsibility for improving performance if they are not prepared to take personal responsibility for finding time to meet. It is as simple as that.

Simplicity Rule 3 'Keep it brief'

Time is precious so there is no point in wasting it. Formal coaching and mentoring sessions in the workplace should be quite productive enough if they take between 30 and 75 minutes. If they are shorter you don't really have time to become focused. However, if sessions take longer they run the real danger of straying into becoming counselling or therapy sessions.

Not everyone will agree with this view. Even in the community context, where extreme patience is required, it is still important to keep a sense of proportion about the time being spent. The workplace, however, is a robust environment and possibly is becoming even more demanding and unforgiving. We do not deny that counselling and therapy have an important role to play here, too, but we do believe that it is a job for specialists and to expect all managers to be able to do it is unrealistic. On the other hand, we do believe that all managers could become good coaches and mentors.

We also acknowledge the need to be flexible in applying this rule. Sometimes, situations are too stressful to be rushed. Sometimes, learners need time to unburden themselves. Certain types of people simply don't respond easily to time-pressured situations. So the coach and mentor have to be willing to be both flexible and patient.

This is where the 'make sure you meet' rule applies. Regular meetings allow the coach–mentor to vary the length of the meetings to take account of the occasional stressful or difficult session. But after, say, three of these necessarily lengthy sessions, we would advise turning to another specialist for help. Coaches and mentors cannot be expected to be able to handle every situation and they become potentially dangerous if they think they should.

Simplicity Rule 4   'Stick to the basic process'

At the most basic level, coaching and mentoring sessions are one-to-one meetings where the learner talks about issues they choose and the coach and mentor listens and asks questions. They need focus, structure and especially good time management. Sticking to a simple process that ensures this happens is therefore crucial. So:

- Ask the learner either to come prepared with their agenda or spend the first few minutes agreeing it.

- Ideally you should both write it down and manage the time spent on each item.

- Agree that taking notes is purely optional.

- However, make certain you both write down any action point that the learner decides they genuinely want to commit to do and make sure it is item one on the agenda for the next meeting.

- Agree the date and time for the next meeting.

The process really is as simple as that. If you stick to it you are signifying to the learner that:

- These are not management, operational or performance review meetings.

- These are not appraisal meetings that require documentation for the Personnel Department.

- These are not disciplinary meetings.

● These *are* meetings which are controlled by the learner and focused on them and their needs and ambitions. In mentoring sessions, they are also meetings which are completely confidential.

Simplicity Rule 5 'Develop the "ask, not tell" habit'

Most managers quickly develop the habit of 'acting as managers are expected to act'. This will vary from organization to organization, depending on the prevailing culture (and probably on how many different training courses managers have attended!). It will also depend on age, gender and personality type, but you can be pretty sure that there will be 'management style habits'.

You can also be reasonably sure that many managers will be unfamiliar with acting as coaches and mentors or fully accepting the underlying philosophy that 'letting go of control = potential for higher performance'. The idea that good coaching and mentoring means moving quickly away from the 'hands-on' to the 'hands-off' position is one of the most difficult barriers for managers to jump.

Developing the 'ask, not tell' habit is a vital new habit for managers and the community volunteer mentor to learn. Spelling it out as the, '80 per cent asking questions and only 20 per cent giving answers rule', is another way we have found that helps some people to adapt their style. Constant repetition and reminders of this rule are probably the most certain ways to get it established.

Even managers who can accept this philosophy intellectually have real practical problems in applying it. Faced with the pressures of accountability for both positive financial and customer satisfaction short-term results, many managers tend to revert to more traditional command and control styles and techniques. To expect otherwise is unrealistic and unsympathetic.

Simplicity Rule 6 'Remember, it's all about learning'

Another real attitude barrier that busy people have to jump is the concept of 'self-responsibility for learning'. A deeply ingrained habit, indeed preference for some people, is to associate 'learning' with classroom or training course activities. Traditionally, organizations have taken primary responsibility for developing the skills and knowledge of their employees. They have also taken responsibility, in many cases, for planning whole careers. The role of the line manager has largely been confined to conducting the annual appraisal and agreeing a 'wish list' of training courses.

Coaching and mentoring sessions on a monthly basis, involving discussing a personal development agenda determined by the learner, will represent a major change of behaviour for a large number of managers. In our experience only about 30 per cent of any management population will, in the short-term, be open to persuasion to try to implement this kind of change in their routines. Even then it will take three to four months before the benefits become apparent, but benefits there certainly will be and patient persistence will be rewarded.

One of the benefits most likely to be noticed first (but often resisted by professional trainers) is the real cost-effectiveness of coaching and mentoring compared to the results of simply sending people on courses away from the workplace. An hour of on-the-job learning and development that can be immediately related to current applications saves a great deal of time and money.

Persistently reminding people that 'it's all about learning' and simply pointing out the real-life benefits helps to make coaching and mentoring become the habitual way 'we do things around here'.

Simplicity Rule 7   'Expect to gain yourself'

Benefits from coaching and mentoring are not a one-way street flowing only in the direction of the learner, the employing organization or the wider community. Coaches and mentors almost always benefit themselves equally by learning new techniques for getting results from the people they work with. There are also the less tangible benefits of the feedback from more highly motivated and appreciative colleagues, or from those who have made real breakthroughs in managing their previously difficult life situations.

Coach–mentors should not be embarrassed to acknowledge the 'self-interest' expectation. Indeed, we would positively encourage them to adopt this win–win attitude. Equally, it is worth emphasizing that our definition of the overall purpose of coaching and mentoring includes 'helping people to become the person they want to be'. This opens the possibilities of rewards from outside the immediate environment of the organizational setting, while, without becoming too idealistic, opens the possibilities also of meeting moral and spiritual fulfilment, too.

Chapter 10

Suggested Additional Learning Options and References

Our subject area has grown so large that it is impossible to list all the learning options that are available or that we would recommend had we been able to use them. What follows, therefore, is a list of just some of the more helpful books we would recommend. We also include sources of other references we have used in this book that are not included in this list.

Blackwell, R (1996) In pursuit of the feel equal factor, *People Management*, June

Carr, R (1999) *Dancing with Roles*, Peer Resources, Compass, Victoria BC

Clutterbuck, D (1991) *Everyone Needs a Mentor*, 2nd edn, Institute of Personnel and Development (IPD), London

Clutterbuck, D (1998) *Learning Alliances*, IPD, London

Clutterbuck, D and Megginson, D (1999) *Mentoring Executives and Directors*, Butterworth, London

Downey, M (1999) *Effective Coaching*, Orion Business Books, London

Dryden, G and Voss, J (1994) *The Learning Revolution,* Accelerated Learning Systems, Aylesbury

Farmer, J (1996) *Workplace Development: mentoring for work-based training*, Department of Education and Employment, London

Forrest, A (1995) *Fifty Ways to Personal Development,* The Industrial Society, London

Fortrang, L (1999) *Take Yourself to the Top*, HarperCollins, London

Gallwey, T (1974) *The Inner Game of Tennis*, Random House, New York

Gallwey, T (1981) *The Inner Game of Golf,* Jonathan Cape, London

Goleman, D (1996) *Emotional Intelligence*, Bloomsbury Publishing, London

Hardingham, A (1998) *Psychology for Trainers*, IPD, London

Harrison, R (1998) article in *People Management*, London

Hay, J (1999) *Transformational Mentoring,* Sherwood Publishing, Watford

Hay, J (1997) *Action Mentoring,* Sherwood Publishing, Watford

Hemery, D (1991) *Sporting Excellence: What Makes a Champion?* Collins Willow, London

Honey, P (1994) *101 Ways to Develop Your People Without Really Trying,* Peter Honey Publications, Maidenhead

Honey, P and Mumford, A (1983) *Using Your Learning Styles,* Peter Honey Publications, Maidenhead

Industrial Society (1995) *Managing Best Practice No. 12 Mentoring*, London

Industrial Society (1999) *Managing Best Practice No. 63 Coaching*, London

Jerome, P J (1995) *Coaching Through Effective Feedback*, Kogan Page, London

Kalinauckas, P and King, H (1994) *Coaching – Realising the Potential,* IPD, London

Kliene, N (1999) *Time to Think*, Ward Lock, London

Kolb, D and Fry, R (1975) *Learning Circle of Experience*, McBer and Co, Boston

Landsberg, M (1996) *The Tao of Coaching*, HarperCollins, London

Lowe, P (1994) *Coaching and Counselling Skills,* Kogan Page, London

Maddern, J (1994) *Accelerate Learning*, Accelerated Learning Centre, Bristol

Mayo, A and Lank, E (1994) *The Power of Learning*, IPD, London

Megginson, D and Baydell, T (1979) *A Manager's Guide to Coaching*, British Association for Commercial and Industrial Education, London

Mulligan, E (1999) *Life Coaching*, Piatkus, London

Mumford, A (1995) *Effective Learning,* IPD, London

Parsloe, E (1992) *Coaching, Mentoring and Assessing*, Kogan Page, London

Parsloe, E and Allen, C (1999) *Learning for Earning,* IPD, London
Parsloe, E (1999) *The Manager as Coach and Mentor*, 2nd edn, IPD, London
Pease, A (1984) *Body Language,* Sheldon Press, London
Senge, P (1992) *The Fifth Discipline*, Century Business, London
Shea, G F (1992) *Mentoring: A Guide to the Basics*, Kogan Page, London
Wilkin, M (ed) (1992) *Mentoring in Schools*, Kogan Page, London
Whitmore, J (1997) *Coaching for Performance,* 2nd edn, Nicholas Brealey, London
Whitmore, J (1987) *The Winning Mind,* Fernhurst Books, Steyning

Other References:

Guest, G (1999) *Building Learning Organizations*, paper to European Consortium of Learning Organizations Conference, Glasgow
Kaye, B L, *Up is not the only way: a guide for career developers* (now out of print).
Mayer, J and Salovey, P (1999) 'Emotional Intelligence' article by Jane Pickard, *People Management*, October Issue European Mentoring Centre, Item House, Burnham, Bucks, UK
Ragins, B R (1999), paper presented to European Mentoring Conference 1999 organized by the European Mentoring Centre and AMED
SMILE, *The SMILE Learning System*, Wolsey Hall, Oxford
Tute, W (1995) *People Management*, IPD

Index

Visit Kogan Page on-line

Comprehensive information on
Kogan Page titles

Features include

- complete catalogue listings,
  including book reviews and
  descriptions

- on-line discounts on a variety
  of titles

- special monthly promotions

- information and discounts on
  NEW titles and BESTSELLING titles

- a secure shopping basket facility
  for on-line ordering

- infoZones, with links and
  information on specific areas of
  interest

PLUS everything you need to know
about KOGAN PAGE

http://www.kogan-page.co.uk